Does Anyone Like Midges?

and 99 other improbable Scottish questions

Does Anyone Like Midges?

and 99 other improbable
Scottish questions

Questions and answers
from the letters page of the
legendary *Exploding Haggis*

Jim Hewitson

Black & White Publishing

First published 2006
by Black & White Publishing Ltd
99 Giles Street, Edinburgh, EH6 6BZ

ISBN 13: 978 1 84502 114 6
ISBN 10: 1 84502 114 2

A CIP catalogue record for this book is available from the
British Library.

Printed and bound by Nørhaven Paperback A/S

*To wee Innes James and Reta, his great-granny.
Between them they have the answers to all the
important questions.*

Contents

Introduction

It was the year of the great Union with England, the Jacobites were understandably restless; it looked as if without a negotiated Treaty of Union there might be war. Into this tense setting in Edinburgh 300 years ago burst *The Exploding Haggis.*

The first edition of the news-sheet was produced in a backroom at the city's Blackadder Close. Within a few weeks the paper began to print a monthly queries column with answers and possible explanations to a vast selection of unlikely Scottish topics supplied by its readers. Certainly no one thought that nearly 300 years later the questions would still be flooding in.

Does Anyone Like Midges? is a compilation of pithy, unlikely and improbable questions and witty, sometimes erudite, often plain daft responses from readers of the publication over the past couple of decades. From the existence of trolls to the reasons for the demise of the Clydeside shipbuilding industry, from the nature of Scottishness to an explanation as to why the home towns of Scottish referees are now omitted from match notes, this is a fascinating snapshot of Scotland and the way it is perceived by both the Scots and the outside world.

All sorts of bizarre questions which have long needed answering are to be found in this publication. Carol Craig recently declared that if Scotland is to take its place in the modern world we must recognise that we are a wee country with our good points – and our bad points.

She might have added our contradictory personality makes us one of the most interesting countries in the world, a suitable case for examination and treatment. Where else could the defiant battle cry of 'Wha's Like Us' be seen to flow from basic insecurity, an inferiority complex and a lack of self-belief? Strip us of our cultural icons, the bagpipe, the haggis and the kilt and what do you find – a naked, hungry, tuneless barbarian? Or perhaps an individual more at ease with his or herself.

Why has the letters page become such a fixture in *The Exploding Haggis*? Well, simply because it is the product of a thousand beautiful, complex, often confused minds who happily and frankly express themselves on every conceivable Scottish topic, and some which, to be honest, are difficult to conceive.

This book may not sparkle with intelligence, knowledge, wit and curiosity but, for anyone who has a love of Scotland and is concerned as much about our hang-ups as our heroes, this collection of correspondence will prove compelling reading.

1
Heroes and villains

ⓒ Shirty with Three Lions

Why do Scottish sports fans, football fans in particular, seem so reluctant to support their mother nation, England, in sporting events for which the Scots have failed to qualify? If the shoe was on the other foot, the English would support the Scots for sure.

Betsy Lugar-Boswell (Ms)
National Association for the Advancement of Anglo-Scottish Relations, Britannia Road, Chipping Ongar, Essex

The fact that Ms Lugar-Boswell has to ask this question displays a very basic misunderstanding of the relationship between Scotland and England, 300 years on from the Union. On the map, in the guidebooks, along with Wales and Ulster, Scotland and England may be shown as one country but we are most certainly not one nation. Whereas, in centuries past, the flags of St Andrew and St George were waved in opposition on the battlefield, they are now brandished in the football and rugby amphitheatres.

The so-called Union of 1707 was, in reality, a takeover of Scotland by a Westminster conglomerate. But, despite the treachery that saw our 'leaders' sell us out, the history, the culture, the heartbeat of a nation which was 2,000 years and more in the making cannot be erased by a few signatures on a piece of paper.

Football is the modern manifestation of the long-standing 'difference' between Scotland, the junior partner in the Union, and England. This distinction should never be underestimated. To ask a Scot to support England is illogical and insulting. Certainly, if the English want to support Scotland, that's just fine but don't expect us to reciprocate.

Philip Sutherland
The Salmond Leap, Banchory, Aberdeenshire

Of course, we shouldn't support England – it makes as much sense to ask a Scotsman to eat his own head as it does to suggest that he should salute the three lions. Isn't it bad enough that we have to suffer the triumphalism of 'British' television without expecting us to pull on an England top and get glassy-eyed at the replays of Geoff Hurst's blooter at the end of 1966 final?

Our illustrious leader at Holyrood, Jack McConnell, has sort of shown the way during last summer's World Cup by declaring that we had no obligation to support England and might support other sides with interesting Scottish connections. However, I fear, Mr McConnell, that road may lead to madness. Do we support Germany because we fought them in two world wars, Holland because we taught them how to play curling, Argentina because we like corned beef, Brazil because their salsa dancers are fit, Iran because we really love bitter and twisted underdogs or Cyprus because we go there on our holidays?

No, let's support Scotland enthusiastically when the opportunity arises whether it's on the football field or in the tiddlywinks arena. The 'mother' nation will manage fine without us. And let it be clear – failure to support England does not amount to active anti-Englishness. The day when England, both on and off the park, achieves sporting success with some dignity and humility might be the day we'll offer some quiet applause. However, I fear that day is some way off.

Barry Buddon
13 Parcel o' Rogues Ave, Kilbirnie, Ayrshire

Until the whingeing Scots realise that all of their imagined problems are not created by we English but are self-manufactured, we will continue to see this narrow-minded, self-centred attitude to sport – which Philip Sutherland is correct in saying is seen as the modern substitute for warfare . . . at least by the Scots.

Perhaps once they realise that, whether they like it or not, they are part of a Greater Britain, then they can have the honour of sharing in the reflected glory of successful English football, rugby, golf, cricket, hockey, athletics and, yes, even tiddlywinks teams which appear on the world stage on a regular basis – unlike the Scots.

I have, on visiting Scotland, found you people to be warm and generous but you have a miserly black spot in your souls, folks, which seems to prevent you enjoying the success of others on the sporting field and elsewhere, especially if those others are English. It's not that the Scots are underachievers but it is time they stopped resenting the procession of English success. We are a bigger nation with a glorious history, sporting and otherwise. God bless!

Rev. Roger Pedant
Bury St Edmunds, Suffolk

Pressure on Scots to support England is undoubtedly media-contrived and I blame the BBC for setting the ball rolling. But why should Scots support England? Is it reasonable to expect the Austrians to support Germany or the Kiwis to support Australia? I think not. It's pure nonsense — Ed.

Dance with the Devil

Did the North Berwick witches have a house band at their sabbats?

Catherine Sark
14 Coven Tree Drive, Haggs Castle, Glasgow

Although the North Berwick witches are unquestionably the most notorious Scottish followers of Satan, covens and sabbats (gatherings of witches) were, if you believe the court records, commonplace in Scotland during the period of the witchcraft frenzy from the 1590s and right through the seventeenth century. During this sad episode, more than 3,000 cases of witch hunting are on record and perhaps as many as 8,000 people were put to the stake.

As well as communion with the devil and all sorts of exotic sexual antics at these get-togethers, the witches (often in reality just poor, lonely old women) are alleged to have participated in joysome frolics with Auld Nick, usually to the accompaniment of the bagpipes and the fiddle. It is said that Satan himself was not averse to getting up and gi'en them a blaw.

Here is Robbie Burns's description of the sabbat at Kirk Alloway in 'Tam o' Shanter' written just half a century after the last Scottish witch was executed at Dornoch. He describes Satan sitting in the corner of the kirk in the shape of a beast:

> To gie them music was his charge:
> He screw'd the pipes and gart them skirl,
> Till roof and rafters a' did dirl.

At weddings and funerals throughout Scotland, despite the cautions from the greybeards of the Reformation, dance bands still had a central role and it would have been surprising if reports of witches' gatherings had not had a musical element.

The sabbats and accompanying frolics were normally held on Friday evening (makes sense after a hard week at the office) and were staged in churchyards or at lonely crossroads or in any other suitable out-of-the-way location.

Abernethy Croan
Witchwatch, The Cauldron, Gallowhill, Hexham, Northumberland

A serving lass called Gellie Duncan, from Tranent, who took part in the sabbats at the old kirk in North Berwick and who was cruelly tortured during the investigation of attempts to sink King James VI's ship in the River Forth by witchcraft, is said to have brought along her Jew's harp to the sabbat to provide some hellish musical accompaniment to the activities. This is the first mention of the instrument in the Scottish annals.

Sally Ostriger
Royal Ghent Coven of Witches, Belgium

If we accept that the witches were the inheritors of the old mysteries of pagan Celtic religion it makes sense that music figured prominently in their activities. The great Celtic festivals such as Samhain and Beltane always seemed to have contained a strong celebratory element with dancing accompanied by music. It is natural then that reports of sabbats, particularly in Scotland, should mention musical activity.

Edwin Bunch
The Scary Wee Cottage, Tarbet, Argyll

All A-Quiver

Is the Royal Company of Archers a Scottish regiment and, if so, do they still use bows and arrows?

Percy Flight
The Auld Doo'cot, St Abb's, Berwickshire

It's an interesting and neat thought that somewhere in the British army there might be a company of bowmen trained to bring down ground-to-air missiles with a deftly released arrow, in the same chivalrous style perhaps as the Polish cavalry charging German tanks during World War II. Alas this is not the case.

The Royal Company of Archers now has over 500 members, grown men, resembling camp extras from Camelot in their colourful and ancient toggery. These noble gents constitute the sovereign's ceremonial bodyguard in Scotland. Scottish blood, or strong Scottish connections, is required before being invited aboard.

The company was revived in 1676 in order to encourage the use of the bow and arrow. The nobility were keen to show off their prowess; this seems to have worked because there are records of archery competitions from St Andrews,

Musselburgh, Aberdeen, Selkirk and Peebles. The company received their charter from Queen Anne in 1706.

However, it was George IV's 'tartan' visit to Edinburgh in 1822 which confirmed their modern role at state ceremonies. The Archers are in evidence at the annual garden party at Holyrood where they provide a guard of honour for the Queen and also have an important role at the installation of Knights of the Thistle at St Giles Cathedral.

Dick Brooman-Bentinck
Membership Secretary, Cherish Scotland Before It's Too Late, Milnathort, Kinross

You wid huv to say that the Royal Company of Archers wi' their fancy uniforms and parades an' a' that tosh is very much a part of the pomp and ceremonial of the tourist city of Edinburgh and on that basis we shouldn't be too critical. They help bring in the Yankee dollar and that's fine. But please, don't gie them more credit than they deserve. The Royal Company of Archers is nothing more than a public school club for nobs, would-be nobs and grown men who like playing wi' bows an' arras; only a tenth of them, the so-called 'active members', have to be strong enough to draw a bow in anger. I was intrigued – but not at all surprised – to learn that the Company has to present the sovereign with three barbed arrows on request and in exchange is endowed with 'perpetual access to all public butts'. Nuf' said! Soon, when the socialist republic of Caledonia is established, we shall be rid of all the nonsensical paraphernalia of bygone ages.

Comrade Dan McLean
Mick McGahey House,
Clartyhole Mews, Dumbarton

Mystery Men

Why are the home towns of Scottish referees no longer included in the match information and programme?

John 'Tiny' McSkimming
The Whistler's Nest Nursing Home, Crianlarich, Perthshire

This is a very good question which has baffled me since the residential identification of referees was dropped in their wisdom by the SFA. The official explanation is that the censorship was introduced at the request of the referees themselves to 'provide a degree of anonymity following various examples of invasion of privacy by the media'.

However, as a young sports reporter in Central Scotland it was one of the constant joys in covering the lower divisions to find that your referee for the day came from such exotic places as Burntisland or Sanquhar or Rosehearty.

It suddenly brought them to life. They ceased simply to be anonymous umpires but real people and invariably their home town had the press box wondering about allegiances. These individuals from far-flung places with strange-sounding names were always much more interesting than 'Mr John Smith (Glasgow)'.

I suppose it was felt by the football authorities that the place of abode of a referee was irrelevant and unnecessary information and really so it should be. And right enough in this crazy damned world where football often seems to take on an importance way beyond reason, it might well have left them open to harassment by media and fans.

Because the truth is that the referee, apart from administering the rules, is a vital component in the overall structure of a football match. He is the person who can be targeted for abuse when your team is playing with leaden boots and no imagination. When you know your boys are taking a helluva beating and there's no way back and you've exhausted your expletives on the opposition team and their supporters, the referee is the safety valve. Some referees are characters in their own right, others play a straight, predictable bat.

But, if his home town is identified, it leaves so much more scope for terracing witticisms. Let's take a fictitious example and see how the fun unfolds. Let our referee be Mr Reg Kelly from Lochgelly. Rhyming possibilities are enormous and include belly, smelly, nelly, telly, Pele, jelly. If you can't get a chant out of that lot you should join John Prescott on the croquet lawn.

People must be protected – we understand that – but there is often a high price to be paid.

Bristow Bofers
Editor, *Off the Crossbar*,
Route One, Naxos, Minnesota, USA

I just knew the media would get the blame for this daft idea of keeping the match officials as faceless, homeless individuals. I write on the advice of my lawyer, only to state that, when I climbed in the kitchen window of our local Grade 1 referee, Arnold Arbiter, it was in the pursuit of truth and justice and in an attempt to get some pix of him in the spa bath with the call girl in Crete. The graffiti which accused him of strange sexual practices and a crazy bias in favour of Alloa FC was already daubed on the kitchen wall when I entered.

Tavish Spike
Sports and Obituaries Editor, *The Auchenblane Bugle*,
Auchenblane, Stirlingshire

Ⓠ Bruce the Linguist

My friend, from Grimsby, insists that the Scottish patriot king, Robert the Bruce, was actually English and spoke only Norman French. This can't be true, surely?

Tranquillo Tennant
The Battlements, Cathcart Castle, Glasgow

Every so often this worn-out old controversy about King Robert's heritage surfaces with, I suspect, supporters and advocates of William Wallace, as the real Scottish patriot of the Wars of Independence, stirring the pot. They just don't seem to be able to accept that Wallace was a second-rate street fighter and it took a man like Bruce, with the resolute powers of the skilled diplomat and strategist, to open the door to freedom.

However, these debates are very encouraging for another reason. If you've ever had any doubt that Scotland remains a nation still with its own unique character, then such exchanges confirm our status. Where else in this United Kingdom, or in Europe for that matter, would such an obscure subject as the mother tongue of a long-dead revolutionary cause sic' a stir?

Some cynics might argue that this only confirms that we are locked in a time warp, introverted, navel-gazers out of touch with the greater realities. Bollocks!! It's an indication that we are conscious of, and care about, our history, our wonderful story which three centuries of Union have failed to tarnish.

Bruce was born at Turnberry Castle in Ayrshire in 1274; his mother, Marjorie, was of Celtic stock and his English-born father was of Norman-French extraction. He would certainly still have spoken the Norman-French of his peers but it is also likely that he spoke Gaelic fluently since it would have been the tongue of his household staff and in use right up the west coast from Galloway to the Highlands at this period. It was through this Celtic matriarchal line that he claimed the throne of Scotland.

At his grandfather's castle at Lochmaben there is a strong likelihood that he heard and used the northern English dialect which was later to become broad Scots and it's reasonable to assume his education also included Latin.

Fiasco Dumbello
Carluke Abbot of Unreason (1954), High Street, Carluke

There seems little doubt that Robert the Bruce was a dab hand at the languages. Ronald McNair Scott, a modern biographer of the patriot king, declares, 'He would have become trilingual at a very early age; an accomplishment most necessary for one who has to draw supporters for his struggle from all three spheres' (Gaelic, Norman French and Lowland 'Inglis').

Just to complicate the matter further Fiasco Dumbello would also be as well to remember that the Normans were not French, not at all. Originally they were Norsemen with a Scandinavian language.

The Bruce family, by the late thirteenth century, must have considered themselves truly Scottish and, although they may have spoken French, they were no more French than the people of Quebec are in the twenty-first century. If his pedigree or his commitment to the Scottish cause was in any doubt, the Community of the Realm, the Scottish power brokers, would have chased him.

Peaches Cavendish
Language Assistant, Tranent College of Medieval Tongues, East Lothian

Mr Grumpy?

Is BBC Radio Scotland's Jim Traynor really the rudest, grumpiest sports phone-in host in Scotland or just a cuddly Airdrie fan?

Patrick Whissell
1690 Firhill Road, Glasgow

Having studied football phone-ins all across Europe, the development of a peculiarly Scottish strain is unquestionably one of your little nation's more interesting sporting phenomena in the twenty-first century. Some of your shows are thoughtful, sympathetic, discursive and balanced. Others are not.

Jim Traynor's programme on BBC Radio Scotland suffers from the same problem as all the others. It caters for a disproportionately high number of Rangers and Celtic fans in Scotland compared with that of other clubs. They call not just from Scotland but from all over the world and seem desperate, how do you say in Britain, to make a horse's ass of themselves. Although he bemoans the Old Firm input and urges supporters of other clubs to call, these exchanges with the fair-minded faithful from the ranks of the Rangers and Celtic supporters have become the meat and drink of the Traynor experience.

To make these phone-ins interesting, there must be confrontation. Jim Traynor is a past master at working up a storm from a puff of wind. What floors the punters is Jim's ability to switch in the blink of an ear from a clever, analytical examination of a complex topic such as football club finances to mud-slinging and gutter abuse. He talks the language of the people and, among the fans, I learn that to have been roundly abused by Jim Traynor, better still, to have him put the phone down on you, is a mark of courage and kudos.

It should be fairly obvious to anyone who listens more than once to this programme that Jim's bad temper, rudeness, male chauvinism, Lanarkshire bigotry, patronising attitude, the feeling that the programme interrupts his life, that he is doing the BBC a favour by turning up on a Saturday and that he would much rather be doing 101 other things are all totally contrived.

According to all my media contacts, Jim is a quiet, self-effacing man who loves football, wishes only good things for Scottish football both at club and national level in the face of what often seems like impossible odds, has a fine working relationship with the other BBC pundits, like the mighty Chick Young and Gordon 'I sclaffed that shot at Wembley' Smith, and is not, as one west of Scotland internet critic has described him, 'a sanctimonious, patronising, narcissistic nobber'.

In a media world across Europe where sycophantic ex-footballers are paid small fortunes to crowd our screens, pushing their own private agendas, it is a joy to have someone on a Saturday who cleverly stirs the pot and does not suffer fools gladly. If you are still doubtful, then listen to the slumber-inducing stuff churned out in the English football phone-ins. You'll never fall asleep during a Jim Traynor phone-in. You may switch off in disgust, email the director general, throw the radio out the window, but you will react – that's a promise.

Dr Alberto Di Cattenacio
Academy of Pseudo Football Science,
via Big Joe Jordan, Milan, Italy

Last Saturday evening I was in a No. 44 bus in Crow Road, Glasgow, when I saw Jim Traynor or at least someone who is his double. I mention this only because this individual gave up his seat up to a sweet old lady. Questions must be asked. To start with, would the moaning, self-opinionated, quasi-fascist Traynor we meet over the airwaves every Saturday ever be found on public transport and, secondly, would he ever give his seat up to an old lady? I think not on both counts. But it was definitely him. The grumpy nyaff from the Saturday phone-in is clearly a fiction.

Atlanta Rump
Exotic Reflexologist, Top Floor Left,
1001 Highburgh Road, Glasgow

Head in the Clouds

Is it true that a Scots scientist won the Nobel Prize for physics by sitting on top of Ben Nevis for several weeks?

Tony Topham
High Pines, Upper Silsbury, Dorset

Professor Charles Wilson, Scots physicist, experimenter and Nobel Prize winner, died in 1959. He was born at Glencorse near Edinburgh and studied at Manchester and Cambridge universities. He is generally regarded as a pioneer of atomic and nuclear physics which impact so forcibly on our world today and he won the Nobel Prize for Physics in 1927, sharing this prestigious award with Arthur Compton.

He was noted for his study of atmospheric electricity, one by-product of which was the successful protection from lightning of Britain's wartime fleet of barrage balloons.

In September 1894, he did indeed spend several weeks in a laboratory which, at that time, existed on the top of Ben Nevis. Later he explained how this mountain-top sojourn had influenced his research, saying, 'The wonderful optical phenomena when the sun shone on the cloud surface on the hilltop greatly excited my interest and made me want to imitate the phenomenon in the laboratory.'

At the Cavendish laboratories in Cambridge Professor Wilson began to study the marvel of the clouds and soon made an important discovery while studying the process of cloud formation. He had designed a cloud chamber in which the tracks of single atoms were made visible as tiny water drops – similar to the process which creates an aircraft vapour trail. The paths of the particles were visible for a moment as white streaks and were photographed giving, for the first time, a convincing demonstration in simple terms that atoms really existed.

Devising this cloud-chamber method of marking the tracks of alpha particles and electrons was his greatest achievement, enabling the movement and interaction of atoms to be followed and photographed. The cloud chamber had an important role in the experiments by Ernest Rutherford and his colleagues while establishing the foundations of nuclear science.

In 1925 Professor Wilson was appointed Jacksonian Professor of Natural Philosophy at Cambridge, a post he held until 1934. But, even in retirement, he was found tramping the hills of Scotland, his head, thankfully for the progress of science, still very much in the clouds.

Professor Alec Tron
Müllerlight Institute for the Study of Very Small Things,
Abba Road, Stockholm, Sweden

⊙ Jolly Hockey Sticks

Is it true that the wild and dangerous Scottish game of shinty is the oldest organised team game in Europe?

Bernard Bolt
Strikesure Drive, Aldershot

It seems very likely that shinty can make a justified claim to being the oldest organised team game in Europe. In the early Irish sagas, Cuchulain, the first-century defender of the ancient province of Ulster and an impressive midfielder, came to Scotland to be educated at the feet of the Warrior Queen Sgathach. While he was here, we learn that, between lessons, he defeated the entire local shinty outfit single-handed which must have been a bit humiliating for the poor Scottish warriors.

This was a kind of double whammy because it was the Irish settlers, probably in the Iron Age, who brought hurling to the Western Highlands of Scotland in the first place along with the Gaelic language and, for hundreds of years, hurling and shinty were effectively the same game. However, in the late 1800s the two games moved apart as Scottish teams got themselves organised with a formal set of rules, dealing with such contentious issues as whether or not to wear kilts. Today, the biggest difference between the sports from the point of view of the casual observer is the fact that, in hurling, the players can pick up the ball.Some would argue that shinty has retained much of the warrior violence that characterised the lifestyle of the early Celtic tribes. It is certainly not a game for the faint of heart. However, supporters will tell you that it is contested far more sportingly than football or rugby and that its reputation for injuries is grossly exaggerated.

There is a vast gulf between the two countries in terms

18

the financial aspects of the game. Hurling attracts huge crowds with the All-Ireland final drawing in up to 70,000 people. Interestingly, within the past few years, France has indicated an interest in shinty with a wee league being set up in the Channel port town of Le Havre. What we need in Scotland now is wider recognition of shinty as an indigenous and vital national sport and not just a couthy novelty.

Tam 'The Hammer' McVitie
Kingussie, Inverness-shire

I hesitate to cross camans with my old friend 'Hammer' McVitie but, to be strictly accurate, the oldest organised team game in Europe is hurling, not shinty. As Tam hinted, hurling was probably taken to the West of Scotland in the first centuries of the Christian period by settlers from Ulster.

Cuchulain, the hero of the Red Branch Gaelic legends of Ulster, is said to have taken to the road as a boy with a 'caman of bronze and a ball of silver'. It seems that Cuchulain was a bit of a tricky character because, in his hurling adventures, he took on and defeated 150 youths of Eamhain by catching the ball between his knees and carrying it over the goal line in this rather unorthodox manner. These were the sorts of skills which he displayed when he visited Scotland.

Shinty was, if you like, an offspring of hurling, developing a slightly different set of rules. Both these sports have been described as a 'free-form' style of hockey. There are many similarities in the sport, of course, but sufficient differences evolved to make a set of compromise rules necessary when the hurlers of Ireland take on the shinty players of Scotland as they now do regularly.

Perk O'Donnell
The Porter's Lodge, University College, Dublin

What folk might not be aware of is that shinty was occasionally used as yet another tool of repression against the long-suffering Highlander. As a privilege, some Highland lairds would graciously let their charges play once a year for a keg of whisky as a New Year bonus while restricting the sport for the rest of the year. It is also recorded that the betrayed MacDonalds of Glencoe played shinty with their murderers on the eve of the infamous massacre. And, according to journalist David Ross, shinty can even be linked to the coming of Christianity to Scotland. An argument during a game in Ireland led to the son of the King of Connaught hitting the son of a courtier of the King of Ireland, Diarmid mac Cerbuill, over the head with his caman and killing him. The young prince fled to Columba for sanctuary but Diarmid removed him by force and put him to death. Columba promptly cast off his curragh for Dalriada and Iona. How that affected the history of Scotland is well established.

Donald P. Grant
Station House, Georgetown, Cayman Islands

Every One a Hero

We are always hearing folk droning on about the epic exploits of Bruce, Wallace, Bonnie Prince Charlie and Jack McConnell but can readers nominate some unsung heroes from Scotland's past?

Cathal Carstairs
Patchwork Place, Riddrie, Glasgow

What a challenge Mr Carstairs has set us. This history of Scotland is replete with characters who have helped shape our wonderfully dark and interesting story but who never really get the credit they deserve. I have compiled my own catalogue of such folk over the years but only today do I have the forum to present some of them. They include:

> John Fergusson, the man who in 1671 set up Scotland's first lottery after first testing the competition on our English cousins. Little did John know what he was letting us in for.

> Edward I, king of England, who was so anti-Scottish he asked to have his bones carried around on campaigns against the Caledonians but who united the divergent interests in Scotland for long enough to allow us to gain independence.

> Borderer Archie Armstrong, sentenced to hang for sheep stealing, whose last wish was to read the Bible with his eyes shut. James VI was so taken with this impudence that he appointed Archie court jester. To his eternal credit, Archie was finally made redundant for giving cheek to the Archbishop of Canterbury.

> The anonymous individual who made a sausage out of Butcher Cumberland, the villain (or English hero) of Culloden, by stealing his sword during a riot at a London theatre in which the Duke of Cumberland, third son of George II, had been caught up.

> Alexander Cruden had a bit of time on his hands so he decided to count the number of words in the Bible. Having discovered that there were 773,692, he then decided to count

the letters which totalled some 3.6 million. A little later, perhaps unsurprisingly, Alex was locked up in an asylum.

The oldest recorded victim of a full-scale battle in Scottish history, William Maitland of Lethington, father of Sir Robert, the poet, lawyer and statesman, who was said to be in his ninetieth year when he died at Flodden in 1513. Get stuck in there, Willie.

David Urquhart, a scholar and adventurer from the Black Isle, who was responsible for the introduction of Turkish baths to Britain after he wrote about them in a travel book in 1848.

The list could fill several volumes but how's that for starters? Unsung heroines are more difficult to come by but there is a case for arguing that every Scottish mother comes into that category.

Freya Bertram
Cosy Neuk Café, Dalnaspidal, Perthshire

The heroes, unsung certainly, that I would like to nominate for Mr Carstairs are the Scots who have helped shape the iconography of England, who have given an identity to the poor souls south of the Border who always seem to struggle to present themselves to the world as a nation in any real sense.

Amazingly that archetypal Englishman, the rotund, red-cheeked agriculturalist John Bull, symbol of Ye Olde

England, roast beef and Yorkshire pud, personification of the Land of Grope and Hoary, was the creation of a Kincardineshire doctor. John Arbuthnott was 'seriously educatit' at the University of Aberdeen and, after a move to London, was appointed physician to Queen Anne. John Bull was a character in a political satire penned by Arbuthnott in 1712. Interestingly this wee bit of fun also contained French and Dutch stereotypes, Lewis Baboon and Nicholas Frog. I'll leave you to guess which was which.

As if that wasn't enough, can you believe that 'Rule Britannia', that stirring, patriotic, quintessentially English anthem, the focus of the Last Night at the Proms and strangely popular with confused Rangers fans in recent years, was written in the eighteenth century by a Borderer like myself, minister's son James Thomson?

Like Arbuthnott, Thomson took himself off to London to seek his fortune where initially he worked as a tutor to the children of well-off families. He wrote plays and poetry. In 1737 he was asked by the Prince of Wales to write a musical extravaganza, one of the hit songs from which was 'Rule Britannia'. It proved an immediate success and is still up there as probably the world's most jingoistic, imperialistic English anthem written by a Scotsman.

It's also worth remembering while we're on this theme that Scotland can also claim credit for inspiring the mascot of the United States – Uncle Sam. In 1961, Samuel Wilson, a patriotic meat packer of the early 1800s, born in America of Greenock parents, was recognised by Congress as the original Uncle Sam, the personification of the United States.

Brother Wilfrid
Order of the Transcontinental Incendiaries, Bus Shelter 23, Muirhouse Road, Edinburgh

A Riveting Performance

I've heard it said that Glasgow once had the toughest theatre audiences in the world, seemingly up alongside the crowd at the Roman Coliseum for bloodthirstiness. Is this an urban myth?

Patsy Player
Under-the-Arches, Menstrie, Clackmannanshire

I assume that Patsy Player is referring to the heyday of Scottish music hall, in the 1940s and 1950s, when she talks about an age of aggressive theatre audiences in Glasgow. However, the performing arts in Glasgow went through difficult times long before the crowds started to flock in.

It would seem that the early anti-theatre lobby was just as enthusiastic in their cause as later audiences were in planking bums on seats and waiting for the curtain to rise.

What could reasonably be described as Glasgow's first 'permanent' theatre, a wooden shed propped up against the wall of the Bishop's Palace beside the Cathedral, was burned to the ground in the mid 1700s by fundamentalists egged on by a famous Methodist evangelist preacher called George Whitfield. He called upon the archangel Gabriel – not on this occasion to blow on his horn – but to smite those who 'frequented the devil in Satan's Playhouse'. Now, that's the sort of theatre name which would have the crowds flocking in these days. Whitfield should not be remembered solely for theatre burning. He set up the Bethesda orphanage in Glasgow.

For over a decade after the burning, landowners simply refused to sell or rent land for the construction of another theatre, clearly reluctant to have 'Christians' with arsonist tendencies rampaging around the city. However, in the 1760s, a theatre opened on the site of today's Central Railway station. Everyone who considered selling land for thespian purposes had realised that the wrath of the Lord and his most devoted followers was likely to descend upon them. The individual who eventually sold the city land, John Millar of Grahamstone, had demanded an exorbitant price and explained his willingness to sell by saying, 'If I am to risk my soul, I am entitled to be well paid for it.'

The new theatre went the way of its predecessor when, on the eve of the first performance, another Methodist preacher told the mob at Anderston Cross that he had dreamed he was in hell where Lucifer toasted the health of John Millar. However, the star of the show, the formidable George Anne Bellamy, saved the cultural day by erecting an improvised stage at the Black Bull Inn, making sure the show would go on. Interestingly, the Black Bull was to become Glasgow's earliest music hall. It is surely worth pointing out that, to this day, hiding in the murky corners of Scottish society, there are those who, given half a chance, would burn or destroy anything that did not match their notions of common decency.

Cynthia Rasp

Author of *Arsonists, Methodists and Culture*,
Houghton-le-Willows, Staffordshire

It would be totally wrong to think that the great music hall era in Glasgow – really the '40s and the '50s – was the period when audiences were at their most demonstrative and aggressive. In 1805, for example, there is a court record of a young man fined heavily for lobbing stones at the stage and orchestra pit during a performance at the old Theatre Royal in Queen Street. Some years later the orchestra pit at the Panopticon Theatre down the road at the Trongate was famously covered with chicken wire to prevent musicians being struck with rotten tomatoes, neeps or even the occasional metal rivet tossed by the discerning audience. The story of the rivets tends to confirm the view that the music halls were a particular draw for the city's thousands-strong army of shipyard workers.

Roy Jackmill
The Back Stalls Pub, Glassford Street, Glasgow

Glasgow music halls – places like the Empire, the Metropole and the Empress – fully deserved their reputation as arenas of apprehension, even alarm, for leading show business personalities of the middle years of the twentieth century. Old-timers like me still recall the night that the affable Des O'Connor fainted on stage at the Empire and had to be cairted off. It is said he passed out simply to escape a viciously critical audience. It was the Empire which carried the remarkable distinction of being known among performers as the theatre which if you could play – and survive – you could go on to play successfully in any theatre in the world — Ed.

Overcharged as Usual

My wife Esmé and I are relative newcomers to North Britain and out to dinner recently we overheard the next table discussing the effectiveness of the Highland Charge? Esmé thinks this must be an element built into the British taxation system. Is she correct?

Dick Ratchet-Pole
Little Ealing, by Lochinver, Sutherland

It's interesting – and encouraging – to find new members of the great Highland community seeking such enlightenment. Indeed, there are many charges and penalties to be faced as a resident of the Scottish Highlands, often described as the last great wilderness area in Europe. Personally I would rate North Lanarkshire as an altogether more wild location but that's another matter. Here in the Highlands we face extra charges for all sorts of day-to-day essentials such as fuel and food because of our relative distance from Scotland's centres of economic activity.

I suspect, Mr Ratchet-Pole, that what you overheard being discussed was not a form of taxation but a method of attack adopted by Highland armies in battle in the 1600s and 1700s and which is said to have astonished and terrified the government forces.

Horatio McGilpen
Drummossie Moor, Inverness-shire

No, the Highland Charge is not a penalty jealously imposed by a distant Hanoverian government on those fortunate enough to live today amongst the most beautiful scenery in the world. The Highland Charge was a military tactic adopted by pro-Stuart forces from the Battle of Killiecrankie in 1689 to the final glorious defeat of the clans at Culloden in 1746.

The charge was a unique phenomenon, recognising as it did the power of modern military technology (i.e. the musket) but cleverly grafting it on to the ancient headlong, blood-curdling charge of Celtic warriors which was recorded by chroniclers as far back as Roman times. Creating the Highland Charge was one of the great achievements of the Jacobite commanders.

Basically the charge was to be made, preferably from

high ground, halting in the midst of the sprint through the heather to fire a round from the muskets before throwing these weapons to the ground, re-forming into a wedge then charging sword-in-hand through the musket-fire smokescreen into the government lines. The reputation of this wall of screaming clansmen closing down on the government ranks as they struggled to reload their own muskets brought regular successes for the clansmen and created an air of foreboding amongst their opponents. Many of the losses sustained by the Covenanters in the 1600s came as terrified men were cut down, having attempted to flee in the face of this startling and ferocious charge.

Had not government forces developed a crossfire technique which caught the running Highlanders in a murderous series of musket volleys, who knows what the outcome might have been at Culloden – despite the hefty disadvantages the Jacobites faced on the day.

Murray G. Lord
The Breakfast Bar, Lay-by 22, near Inverurie,
Aberdeenshire

The Highland Charge was a military tactic which, in football parlance, would be called Route 1 (with modification) – a long ball down the middle held up just briefly to allow the midfield to race through in support. It is one of the great regrets of some Scottish football fans, including myself, that this technique with a big striker as target man laying the ball back to the onrushing midfielders has all but been abandoned by the current Scottish team. Neat triangular inter-passing looks good but you cannae beat the high ba' tae a big Joe Jordan character. Sadly, remembering the poor clansmen mown down at Culloden, the day of the big charge on the

Scottish football field – as on the Scottish battlefield – may now be over.

Kirk Berstane
The Photo Booth, Tesco's Supermarket,
Maryhill Road, Glasgow

We are obliged for Murray Lord's rather partial view of the Highland Charge. In fact, the charge is first reported in Ireland in the mid 1600s, introduced by the almost legendary Catholic war chief Alasdair MacColla who brought the tactic with him when he joined the campaign of James Graham, Marquis of Montrose, against the Covenanters. In reality the engagements between the Jacobites and government forces were, as one historian has commented, 'a contest between an undisciplined, archaic host and a disciplined thoroughly modern force'. The Highlanders fused the ancient and early modern tactics with their 'volley and charge' tactic and this audacious but remarkably successful approach has intrigued military historians ever since.

Professor Scintias Gilp
Centre for the Study of Mad Celtic Attacks,
London Road, Cloneakilty, Cork, Ireland

Stone Mad

My friends in Amsterdam insist that the sport of curling, which I have always regarded as a truly Scottish pastime, actually originated in the Netherlands. Is this possible?

Calum Baez
Pluscarden, Moray

If you've ever wondered why curling is called the 'roaring game' then here's the answer. Some folk will tell you it's because of the noise the curling stone makes, especially out of doors on a still frosty morning, as it slides across the ice. However, it also gets its name from the roars of derision issuing from Scottish curlers who are constantly forced to listen to this nonsense about the flatlanders having invented the game.

Here are the facts. During the Middle Ages, there were strong commercial ties between Scotland and the Low Countries. There can be no doubt that this relationship also included an interchange of ideas. The Scottish merchants and seamen who had been playing the game for centuries took the idea to the continent. The fact that the Hollanders were second-raters and poor imitators is surely evidenced by the fact that historians confirm that they played the game with frozen clods of earth. How cheap and nasty is that? Can I also just mention in passing that Scotland are the current world men's 'fours' champions? And where are the Dutch curlers when it comes to these major world tournaments? Nowhere, that's where. I rest my case.

Rory Frost
Mill Pond, Lochmaben

It is clearly time you Scots accepted that the Low Countries are the cradle of curling. I need only point you in the direction of two works by the illustrious Flemish artist Pieter Breugel painted between 1525 and 1529. These paintings, *Winter Landscape with Skaters and a Bird Trap* and *The Hunters in the Snow*, quite clearly show a primitive form of curling taking place. The continent was an altogether more sophisticated place in the sixteenth century and it makes sense that the

Scottish traders would take this sport back to Scotland with them. Never has it been shown that curling stones found in Scotland pre-date this era. In addition it seems to be in the nature of the Scots to claim credit as originators of everything from golf to television. We should not be surprised that they also claim curling as their own.

Ed van Dick
President, Royal Dutch Independent Curlers, Assen, The Netherlands

The evidence that we Scots inventet the game of curling is to my mind overwhelmin'. It was, so the records tell us, the sport o' the people at a time when the nobs preferred the hunt and the Dutch were too busy crowding into their new towns and cities.

Curling originated, and largely stayed within, Scotland's agricultural community. As Robin Welsh has written, 'When the plough was frozen in the furrow the farmers took to the ice.' Persistent attempts by the Dutch to deprive the ordinary working Scot o' credit for giving the world the game of curling are despicable and clearly part of the greater plot by the growing and menacing Euro middle-class to marginalise ordinary working people on the continental periphery.

Comrade Dan McLean
Mick McGahey House, Clartyhole Mews, Dumbarton

Land o' Burns

Was Scotland's national bard Robert Burns a complete waste of space as a farmer?

Edwin Burnes
Moose Jaw, Saskatchewan, Canada

The answer, Edwin, has to be a resounding, 'Sadly, we'll never really know.' Too many distractions – usually involving drink, women and poetry – got in the way of his efforts at farming to allow for a proper assessment. Certainly our national bard had the pedigree to make a go of farming, coming, as the majority of Scots still did in the mid eighteenth century, from an agricultural background. And the family's poverty meant that Robbie – a clever scholar by all accounts – was out at an early age earning his living as a ploughboy in spring and a shepherd in summer.

It has certainly been argued convincingly that much of the inspiration for his early poetry came from these labours on the land. Agriculturalists might say that he spent rather too much time observing nature to bring his labours to profitability. After his father died in 1784, Burns and his younger brother Gilbert took on the farm of Mossgiel, near Mauchline in Ayrshire. This may have been difficult land to work but 'want of success' and relationship difficulties soon had Burns thinking of leaving his native country. However, scholars agree that some of his best poetry was conceived as he drove the plough over the leas of Mossgiel.

K. L. Bonnet
Lapraik Mansions, Ayr Road, Kilmarnock

When Burns moved into literary circles first of all in his home area and then, more spectacularly, among the society folk of Edinburgh, he seemed happy to accept the handle of the Ploughman Poet. Unquestionably he knew the power of public relations in finding sponsors and selling his work in the smart Edinburgh society, which he sought to impress. But did he still genuinely see himself as a man of the soil? Certainly, Burns, despite this literary success, seems to have regularly expressed a desire to return to the plough. Scholars have suggested that he had probably forgotten the hard, relentless graft involved in farming but hankered after 'the simple toil and homely life' of rural Scotland. He was a Romantic, after all.

Clarinda Irvine
Curator of the Burns Collection, Mongolian Museum of Fine Art, Ulan Bator

Patrons re-established Burns on the 100-acre Ellisland farm in Dumfriesshire after his Edinburgh escapades and with the money remaining from his publications he bought stock. With a fifty-seven-year lease and modest rental, everything was set fair and there is no doubt that Burns enjoyed the romantic reconnection with the land – putting his hand to the spade and plough again and wandering his own grounds.

However, the sad truth is that the flattery and easy living of Edinburgh society did appear to have softened him because he quickly began to resent efforts made to get him to attend to the business of the farm. He was, according to an early biographer, Robert Heron, 'addicted to convivial excess' although, during this period, his intellectual powers seem to have burned as bright as ever. Robert Burns might indeed have made more of farming if the muse and cupid hadn't got in the way.

Rev. Johnny Souter
The Manse, Jean Armour's Way, Mount Oliphant, Jamaica

2
Mince and clapshot

Mistaken Identity

Am I right in thinking that crannog is a rather exotic Scottish dessert made from oatmeal and honey?

Myrtle Goff
Parsifal, Fatty Arbuckle Road, Oldham

Some basic confusion here, I think. A crannog, contrary to Myrtle's information, is not a dessert but a highly specialised form of prehistoric dwelling, a defensive homestead, generally found on rocky outcrops or artificially constructed islands of piled rubble and timber frame along the loch shores of Scotland and Ireland. They are unique and remarkable constructions which seem to have been popular on and off over a period of several thousand years. A few were in use right through to the 1600s as hunting and fishing bases and a number of Scotland's medieval castles are thought to have been constructed on crannog sites which were, of course, symbols of power, prestige and wealth.

Normally the crannog consisted of circular timber frameworks with piles driven into the bed of the loch. Some were reinforced with stone. Jetties and harbours can be traced. Occasionally the crannogs had shallow underwater causeways to land but most may have had timber walkways. The generally held view is that they were built to provide sanctuary from raiders in troubled times and as protection for people and domestic animals from wild animals, probably most often wolves, bears and wild boar. The most intense period of occupation seems to have been the Iron Age.

The cold water of the lochs has preserved timbers, seeds, plants and wooden utensils and this allows a clear picture of how the occupants lived. These roomy dwellings might have housed up to twenty people and were probably thatched with reeds. Archaeological evidence suggests that the crannog people ate well, cultivated crops and looked after domestic animals. One enigma of the crannogs is that the people, at least in Loch Tay, did not appear to fish. Some scholars have suggested that this may be due to the fact that certain species of fish, for example the salmon, may have held a special place in the religion and traditions of the loch dwellers.

Rev. Alec Bell
Underwater Archaeology Unit, Free-Range Church of
Caledonia, Campbeltown, Argyll

Your exotic sweet is without doubt cranachan which is produced in a variety of different ways but generally is a delightful mix of oatmeal, cream, honey, whisky and raspberries. As it is presented today cranachan seems an unlikely dessert for the ordinary agricultural workers of Scotland in times past. However, apparently it was originally a summer dish consumed around harvest time. The traditional manner of eating was by bringing dishes of each ingredient to the table for self-assembly to taste.

It was sometimes called a 'crowdie cream' because a soft cheese was used instead of cream and another version was the 'ale crowdie' with ale, whisky and treacle among its ingredients. At Halloween it is recorded that wee charms were placed in the mix.

Toasted pinhead oats, fruit and cream would be laid out alongside the lubricants, whisky and honey.

It does take a little leap of the imagination to visualise our Bronze Age crannog dwellers tucking into something quite as sophisticated and trendy as the modern cranachan but on the other hand they appear to have had all the necessary ingredients bar the whisky which is thought to have been brought to Scotland by the early Celtic monks in the first centuries AD. However, we now think these Bronze Age dwellers may have produced a wine from sloe berries, so a form of cranachan in the crannogs is not beyond the bounds of possibility.

Peter Pinhead
Just Desserts, Back Road, Bridge of Orchy, Argyllshire

If you're looking for examples of the crannog, Loch Ness, Loch Awe and Loch Tay are probably the best locations. In Scotland upwards of 400 crannog sites have been identified and Loch Tay alone boasts eighteen crannogs from the late Bronze and Early Iron Age. At Kenmore on Loch Tay archaeologists at the Scottish Crannog Centre have constructed the first crannog to be seen in Scotland since the time of Christ — Ed.

Packing 'Em In!

How many wolves and bears are thought to still remain in the mountains of Scotland?

Wan Lang Fang
Bamboo Garden Cantonese Restaurant,
The Esplanade, Arbroath, Angus

Having noted Mr Fang's address, my first concern on reading his query was that perhaps his restaurant is seeking imaginatively to broaden their menu from stir-fired smoked kippers to more exotic dishes. However, we have to disappoint you. Bears have been absent from Scotland for perhaps more than 1,000 years. The Romans were known to have taken Caledonian bears for bloodthirsty gladiatorial battles in arenas of the Empire.

The wolf is a much more recent loss – the last Scottish animal was killed in either 1680 (by Sir Ewen Cameron of Lochiel) or in 1743, according to a more detailed record. On this occasion, the wolf in question was reputed to have been the last man-eater. It had waylaid and eaten two children of a poor woman on the lands of Moy south of Inverness.

When word was brought to the Chief of the Mackintoshes, he called on the clan to hunt down the wolf. Everyone turned out to the muster except Eagan MacQueen, the laird's ghillie, a huge man 'nearer seven than six foot'. Mackintosh was enraged at this defection but, as the hunt got under way, MacQueen appeared and asked, 'What's the hurry?' before producing the severed, bloody head of the wolf from beneath his plaid.

To be truthful we're not even sure if the Moy wolf was the last in Scotland. As late as 1756, Lord Morton, the President of the Royal Society, claimed that the wolf was still present in Scotland in some numbers. Sources of this information are unidentified but perhaps wild dogs may have been mistaken for wolves.

In recent years, there has been talk of reintroducing the wolf into the Highlands but it's doubtful whether the wolves would co-operate and restrict themselves to devouring deer from the numerous herds instead of turning their attention to easier targets like sheep and perhaps the odd hill walker.

Ursula Lycan
Head Keeper, Pittodrie Bear Pit, Aberdeen

How bothersome that your journal should see fit to raise again the possibility that wolves might be brought back to the Scottish mountains and glens. This daft idea had run its course and the loony wildlife fringe had moved on to softer targets. Now, all you will do by printing Mr Fang's query is to bring the topic back to prominence. There is one powerful reason why the wolf will never return voluntarily to the Scottish hills. Whether the last wolf was slain in 1680, 1743 or later is irrelevant. The fact is that the Scottish hills have changed dramatically in the past two and a half centuries. It is estimated that we probably now have only about one per cent of the tree cover that was available to the wolf in the mid 1700s. It simply isn't the sort of environment where wolves would prosper.

Gavin Todd
Milton of Loarn, Morayshire

Talking of the absence of wolves from the Scottish mountains, it's important not to overlook the fact that Scotland in common with many European countries, most notably France, may no longer have any bona fide wolves but has a tradition of werewolves. Experts believe this superstition – that some humans have the magical power to transform themselves into the shape of a wolf – probably originates with the pagan worship of animal spirits where the shaman or witch doctor would dress in a wolf mask or skin.

It seems likely that the myth of the werewolf arrived in Scotland in the baggage of invading Norsemen. Some claimed Scandinavian kings could turn themselves into wolves. However, the legend persisted throughout the Middle Ages, with the wolf being equated with the devil and hence with all that it was evil, and this belief carried through into the modern era. In the Borders, apparently, a destructive blouster of wind was called a 'wolf wind'. And, of course, there's the man/wolf which inspired Robert Louis Stevenson's classic study of dual personality, *The Strange Case of Dr Jeykll and Mr Hyde*.

Just as some poor souls believe they are vampires, it seems that occasionally people manage to convince themselves that they are werewolves. Around the time of the First World War, a hermit-shepherd in Inverness-shire was rumoured to be a werewolf. As in the days of the witchcraft frenzy, lonely, isolated non-conformists often become the targets of suspicion, accusation, then persecution.

Perhaps then it's just possible that there are still wolves – or at least half-wolves – in the Scottish glens.

Bobbie Patton
Dept of Social Anthropology,
West Dunbartonshire Council, Renton

Oat Cuisine

While visiting friends in Kirkcaldy, I offered to cook the breakfast porridge only to be told in whispered tones that porridge making was an almost secret art and should only be performed by the master of the house. Can this possibly be true? I was also told that, after hundreds of years as a Scottish staple, oatcakes have only recently been given the royal seal of approval.

Anton McNeish
1 Grainstore, Dunfermline, Fife

If there is one topic apart from football that can have the Scots at each other's throats it is the various techniques and ingredients for making a traditional plate of porridge. The truth is that there are almost as many ways of producing a plate of porridge as there are Scots to eat it. But let's get one myth out of the way from the outset – not all Scots like porridge. In fact, I know folk who positively abhor the dish – I once heard it described as Ready Brek for adults. This abhorrence almost certainly stems from generations of Scots who were force-fed grey, menacing slabs of porridge textured with as much salt as the body could stand. Made properly, porridge is a sheer delight. Try it as Queen Victoria did with a splash of cream and a raspberry.

The oatmeal art is a very serious affair and debate can be angry and extensive. But, these days, responsibility for making porridge is certainly not the exclusive right of the father of the house – although there may be some reactionary porridge makers out there, as Anton found.

One American professor declared in 2001 that the best way to get an authentic tang to your porridge was to heat the mixture on a peat fire alongside a pair of sweaty socks. For their part, the revisionists insist that your porridge mix should be microwaved in a plastic bowl. My grandfather swore that the only porridge worth eating had been poured three days previously into a kitchen drawer and allowed to solidify before being cut out in slices. It was advisable to have the drawer well scrubbed before pouring in a pot of porridge.

Whatever way it's made, porridge is formidable gear and liable to put hairs in places where hairs really shouldn't be.

Aloysius Snib
'Porridge for the People Campaign',
Couthy Street, Auchtermuchty

Oatcakes were originally the snack of the Scots soldier in the field. The recipe was not complex – oats and water. If we are to believe the oatcake propaganda of the past decade, it is good for your heart and for the male sex drive. This perhaps explains why, in Victorian times, university students would humph a bag of oatmeal to their digs and bake their own oatcakes before heading off to the beer bar.

Your friends are right about the much-delayed royal seal of approval for the oatcake. It was as recently as 2002 that the oatcake, which seems to have been around forever, was officially recognised. Walkers of Speyside were appointed official suppliers to the Queen. Apparently the Queen likes to spread marmalade on her oatcake. Always popular in the old Commonwealth, oatcakes are now catching on in Europe. Are we at all surprised to learn that half the population of England when surveyed had never heard of the oatcake, never mind having tasted one? They don't know what they're missing.

Noble Ptarmigan
Inchworthy Path, Shotts, Lanarkshire

Like our whisky, the key to a good oatcake is our magical Scottish water — Ed.

Northern Exotica

What is the origin of the strange Orkney dish called clapshot which we were offered and tasted while on holiday in the north?

Barbro Edfors
Neapgarten 80, Stockholm, Sweden

Sometimes a dish and an accompaniment go together as if nature had intended them to share a plate. Clapshot can be eaten with almost anything but is quite simply a joy when devoured with haggis.

Clapshot is simplicity itself. The Orkney bard, the late George Mackay Brown, once gave the formula for this dish – 'tatties and neeps boiled together – then mashed with a goodly dollop of butter and eaten hot with plenty of pepper and salt'. It has also been made with lashings of pepper, suet and chives. As the *Glasgow Herald*'s Willie Hunter once elegantly remarked, 'With haggis it causes the rarest of food chemistry by which the total dish becomes immeasurably greater than the sum of its parts.' Haggis, he believed, was indeed the great chieftain but clapshot was his indispensable loyal lieutenant.

Its classic presentation is, therefore, with haggis but it is a delight taken with everything from cheese to corned beef, from sirloin steak to sausages – in truth it goes with just about anything. I have never met anyone who has tried fish and clapshot or a fried egg and clapshot but there is surely absolutely no objection to these combinations. Once again the great Orcadian GMB suggested that the perfect accompaniment for this dish is a glass of home brew.

There are some who will argue for clapshot as a fabulous food for relieving stress and tired limbs but again I have no personal experience of this phenomenon. However, it is easy to imagine its curative properties when you see the steam rising from the golden yellow mash, a knob of butter melting luxuriously in its centre. A joy, a delight.

Tom Turbot
Mill on the Flaws, Huntingdonshire

There is really no point getting overexcited about clapshot and its place in the Scottish heritage. The facts are pretty straightforward. Much as Orcadians, who value the dish so highly, would like to believe it was brought here by the Norsemen, this theory has to be set aside. Potatoes, as far we can tell, only reached Orkney in the late 1600s and turnips into the following century. That this dish does have its origins in the north is confirmed to a certain extent by the fact that, although haggis is so nobly celebrated in the work of Robert Burns, there is not a single mention of clapshot.

Effort Handler
Pennywise, Forth Parade, Portobello, Edinburgh

A Tern for the Worse?

Did seabirds ever form an important part of the Scottish diet?

Ramsay Nairn
Head Bottle Washer, Macrahanish Academy of Food
Sciences, Argyll

In days of great shortages on the land, for example in times of famine, Scots who lived near enough to the coast would look even more enthusiastically towards the sea for their sustenance. Fish and shellfish could be taken from the ocean and shore to help a hard-pressed family through another winter. And birds and/or their eggs could be gathered from the cliffs to supplement diets but clambering around above the waves was always dangerous work.

Seabirds interestingly are longer lived and breed later than land-based birds. The fact that they nest in colonies in numbers from a few dozen to many millions has meant that they were always an attractive option for both winged predators and humankind. Nesting as they do on high sea cliffs they are also particularly vulnerable to the vagaries of the Scottish climate – they might experience warmth and clear, peaceful skies one day then, when the icy wind picks up and whips across the islands, they are driven from their nesting sites.

There are some 250 species of seabird but they represent only three per cent of the world's total bird population. As well as having their eggs taken and being eaten, seabirds were also caught for feathers and oil for use in the cruisie lamps on the long northern winter nights. One of the saddest, terminal losses from such exploitation was the extinction of the three-foot-high great auk, a flightless bird of the same scale as an emperor penguin, the last bird in the British Isles being killed in Papa Westray, Orkney, in the early 1800s. It was hunted to extinction for its beautifully soft feathers.

Lofty Spitzbergen
Leading Ornithologist, Greenock Technical College Trans-Antarctic Expedition (1921–24).

It's amazing how some traditional stories come to be regarded as mere myths or legend. Such is the case with the puffin. Tales of the St Kilda islanders cooking up the coulter nebs in their porridge have long been regarded as mere fantasy. However, there seems to be every possibility that this is true. Nineteenth-century Wigtownshire polar explorer John Ross declared that he found puffin 'excellent, even in a pie. It has been overlooked by everyone that the fishy flavour is confined to the fat, the whole of which is lodged immediately under the skin and is chiefly situated on the haunches. The muscles are always free of any oily or rancid fishy taste.'

Puffins, of course, are a protected species today, as are so many other seabirds, so really they shouldn't be found on the dinner table. However, it is widely known that, given half a chance, Icelanders in particular, who are said to eat just about everything that flies, swims or walks, will rustle you up some smoked puffin, which connoisseurs tell me bears a stunning resemblance to smoked salmon.

The eating of seabirds in Scotland may be a thing of the past but there seems to be no doubt that a major element of the diet of coastal dwellers in centuries past came from the cliffs. The eating of puffins is also interesting because an old Vatican edict once classified puffins as fish, allowing them to be put on the menu on Fridays.

Albert Scarfie
The Cliff Edge, Cape Wrath, Sutherland

A good example of seabirds as an integral part of the diet can be found in the Scottish social histories which describe how the gannet, or solan goose, found in vast numbers on the rocky outcrop of the Bass Rock in the Forth Estuary, was sold to the citizens of Edinburgh where it made regular appearances on dinner tables. Cormorants and black-headed gulls are reported to have an interesting, fishy flavour — Ed.

Fangs for the Memory

I was told by a newspaper vendor in Aberdeen's Union Street while on holiday that Count Dracula came from Cruden Bay. Is vampirism a particular problem in Scotland?

Eck 'The Tooth' Finlay
Bathgate Road, Brora

Information from newspaper sellers I have discovered over the years, whether they're in Aberdeen, Edinburgh, Glasgow or Dundee, is about as useful as their horse-racing tips. Mind you, on the topic of Dracula, Eck, your vendor wasn't too far off the mark.

Before we venture down the dark, scary passageways of vampirism we should remember two important facts. Firstly, Count Dracula was modelled by writer Bram Stoker on a real-life character, Vlad the Impaler, and, secondly, inspiration for the *Dracula* setting in a spooky castle almost certainly came from now-derelict Slains Castle near Cruden Bay, Aberdeenshire, where Stoker spent summer vacations around the turn of the twentieth century.

Sadly, some poor misguided souls, having read *Dracula* or more usually nowadays having been entranced by vampire movies, see themselves as the undead, condemned to wander the world forever as the agents of Satan, feasting on human blood.

Are there not enough problems in this crazy world without creating more for ourselves? The vampire is a myth. What we are left with after examining all the legends from Vlad to the present day is the conclusion that, as a species, we are just bloodthirsty.

Carmilla James
Author of *Dracula Sucks – Destroying the Vampire Legend*,
Dental Hospital, Sauchiehall Street, Glasgow

I have read that, in 1895, while staying in the Kilmarnock Arms hotel in Cruden Bay, Bram Stoker had a particularly vivid nightmare after devouring a plate of dressed crab. No surprise there, you might think. However, that has to have been one of the most productive nightmares in history. The following morning, he jotted down the first five chapters of the work he titled *Dracula*. Apart from the crab special, the other main source of inspiration was said to be the gaunt cliff-top shell of Slains Castle, the ancestral home of the Earls of Errol.

What is interesting for me is that the Stoker connection with Cruden Bay, although it has become world famous, is far broader. He wrote short stories with the village as the setting and quite openly told friends that the district provided him with great inspiration.

Rosa Tufen
Castle Alucard, Transylvania,
Somewhere in Central Europe

Among people like myself who know a lot about literature there is no debate. The first five chapters of *Dracula* by Bram Stoker are among the most descriptive and evocative in the English language. The town of Whitby in Yorkshire also has a claim on Stoker but there is no doubt in my mind that the Cruden Bay coast and Slains Castle in particular were a potent inspiration for the writer.

I also have my own theory as to why his story of vampires still rings true more than a century after it was written. Among us in the Scotland today of electronic messaging, renewable energy and smoking bans are people who believe themselves to be vampires. Since drinking blood still borders on being socially unacceptable, many modern 'vampires' have convinced themselves that their sharp incisors and bloodshot eyes are just part of their confused genetic make-up and not the result of a love bite in the soft flesh of the neck.

Professor Paul Moriarty
Dept of Clever Joined-Up Words, University of Glen Affric,
Perthshire

Buchan Blues

We were interested to find on a visit to the north-east that Peterhead is known as the 'Blue Toon'. Try as we might, we could not discover the reason for this nickname. Can you help?

Peaches Cavendish
Grays Creek, Middlemarsh, Connecticut, USA

Peterhead has a prison, a serious drugs problem, a decimated fishing fleet and yet some of the most kind-hearted and genuine people you are likely to meet anywhere in Scotland are to be found there. The nickname of the 'Blue Toon' has been the source of discussion over many years and, while I have studied this phenomenon at length, I have yet to come up with a definitive answer.

However, there are perhaps a few explanations which can be immediately dismissed. The local Peterhead football club do indeed have a blue and white team strip but this may have resulted from the nickname rather than having been the source of it.

On the same theme the Blue or Bloo Toon does not get its name because it is filled to overflowing with supporters of Rangers, the Glasgow team noted for their blue associations. There are indeed busloads of Rangers supporters in Peterhead but that other Glasgow giant, Celtic, also has many fans in the town. Rather depressingly they probably outnumber the Aberdeen supporters in the town. Equally there is no suggestion that the Blue Toon, which has its share of satellite dishes, gets its name because of a particular liking among the townsfolk for pornographic literature or erotic TV programmes. Peterhead is sexy but it is not the porn capital of the north-east.

Nor, despite the trials which the town has faced in the past few decades, can we say that Peterhead is blue because the folk are stressed and depressed. There are problems but you are very likely to receive a memorably warm smile in the paper shop or at the bus stop from old and young alike.

Mauve Purdy
Tanorama, Sunnyside Street, Peterhead

The first, and many think the most likely, explanation for the nickname of 'Blue Toon' relates to Peterhead's geographical position . . . right out on the north-eastern point of the Scottish mainland. According to the received wisdom, Peterhead is held to be 'an afa' caul place'. On an exposed coastline, surrounded by the North Sea, gales whip in mercilessly and folk bend into the wind in Harbour Street as they go about their daily business. Blue from the cold – it's possible.

The second multifaceted explanation relates to the architecture of the community. The buildings are constructed from granite with a silvery bluish tinge and the roofs are covered with bluish slate. Add to this the street lighting which has a bluish glow then perhaps we have come close again to explaining the sobriquet. Others have suggested that uniforms – official and unofficial – seen in and around the town are distinctively blue. Fishermen and fish process workers tended to wear blue smocks and blue gear while prisoners at Peterhead jail had a blue uniform.

For a century from the late 1700s, Peterhead was a centre for the whaling industry with thousands of tons of blubber being landed annually and boiled down in huge vats by the quayside at Keith Inch where there were three boil yards. Whalers and their families lived amongst this 'aromatic' activity and the process, as well as giving off an atrocious smell, is said to have dispersed a thin blue haze over the town. For many, this seems the most logical explanation for the nickname.

Professor Alex 'Tricolour' McGowan
School for Studying Scottish Colours, Rainbow Avenue, Cathcart, Glasgow

Cause for Celebration

Why is St Andrew's Day such a downbeat event in the homeland when, like Burns Day, it is celebrated with enthusiasm by Scots communities all over the world?

Bill Budge
The Kettle Yarn, 60 Tinbarra, New South Wales

Every so often, for the past 400 years, the lobby for greater recognition of St Andrew's Day has sprung into life. However, there are many who believe that, until Scotland gains her independence, the anniversary will never be properly recognised.

One of the greatest enigmas in Scotland's story is the fact that the great Scottish nation in exile, the Scots diaspora if you like, does indeed celebrate the saint's day with far more enthusiasm than folk at home seem prepared to do. It does often appear that, as the old maxim has it, the further we are from the homeland, the more vigour we put into the celebration of the patron saint or our national bard.

I think there might be good reasons for this. For the exiles in particular, the saltire represents not only the saint but the home ground. For a few hours in the most unlikely corners of the globe, you can wrap yourself up, either literally or figuratively, in the auld flag. Like the whisky and the endless choruses of 'Scots Wha Hae', the flag and the saint help to build a spiritual bridge to Scotland. What is going on in Scotland I'm afraid I'll have to leave to someone closer to home.

Larry Pickup
TeDoon Kamp, Transvaal, South Africa

It is a sad fact that most countries celebrate their national day with much more enthusiasm than we do. There does seem to be an odd reluctance to grasp St Andrew's Day and make it into a genuine national day. Reasons for this lukewarm attitude of home-based Scots to their saint's day are complex, I think, but interesting.

I believe an increasingly important factor has been the ridiculous expansion of the Christmas shopping period. The frenzy now begins in November – some might say October – but, certainly by the end of the eleventh month, Scots are well and truly tuned in to the Christmas frequency and saints' days have to take a back seat. An additional element is also probably the wild charge to Hogmanay and the fact that, by the end of January, we are celebrating Robert Burns' birthday which has established itself in the past 200 years as one of the watershed days of the Scottish calendar. These months between November and February are already crowded with social activity and it is difficult for our saint's day to grab the limelight.

One solution to this problem might be to have a winter festival beginning on 30 November and stretching through the Christmas/New Year period, ending on the bard's birthday. Scottish National Party leader Alex Salmond has been one of the leading proponents of this idea. However, to succeed this will require the consistent and enthusiastic support of all parties in the Scottish Parliament.

But there are other, perhaps more subtle, factors feeding into this equation. Looking a wee bit deeper, I wonder if this coolness is a Calvinistic echo of the rejection of sainthood and the worship of relics which brought us St Andrew in the first place.

Brother Wilfrid
Order of the Transcontinental Incendiarists, Bus Shelter No. 23, Muirhouse Road, Edinburgh

At the moment, there seems to be an elitist, establishment feel to the St Andrew's Day celebrations that do take place – auld geeks fae the Order of the Thistle parading about on the cobbles wi' their feathered berets and Dracula cloaks. Until the day is properly democratised, made into a true festival of the people, it is unlikely ever to capture the public imagination.

Comrade Dan McLean
Mick McGahey House, Clartyhole Mews, Dumbarton

Andrew was martyred in Greece on 30 November AD 69 and I have occasionally wondered if the problem might be that we actually got so little of Andrew. His spirit may live amongst us but the most we got of his physical being was a rickle o' banes. Apparently an angel told St Regulus (supposedly an assistant of Columba) to carry the saint's remains to the ends of the earth. Now where did he end up – was it Fulham or Fiji or Famagusta? – no, indeed, it was Fife. Regulus, who presumably had a light luggage allocation, brought only a tooth, an arm bone, a kneecap and some fingers.

I understand the Scottish Executive is still giving a lot of thought to a national holiday on St Andrew's Day, looking over their shoulder at Ireland where St Patrick's Day, with a programme packed with events brings in between £60m and £135m to the national economy – food for thought. Perhaps the example of France is worth thinking about. Instead of a national holiday, let each Scots resident give up a day's pay to help a nationally agreed cause.

But it is indeed amazing to think that, when you are halfway through St Andrew's Day in Fife or Falkirk, everyone in places like Auckland and Wellington will be in their beds, having already had their St Andrew's Night dinners. In Melbourne and Wagga Wagga, they'll be clearing away the plates while in Vancouver and Los Angeles they will just be waking up at the start of another St Andrew's Day. It truly is a worldwide phenomenon.

Digby St Clair
Plout Kirn, Den Bosch, The Netherlands

First of all, I like the way auld Digby wi' a Dutch address is volunteering 'resident' Scots to give up a day's pay instead of having a national holiday.

Am I the only who thinks that St Andrew's connection with Scotland is pretty dodgy and circumstantial and that this is where the problem in the nation's apparent coolness towards our patron saint might lie? Perhaps it's high time we started looking seriously at alternatives. There are a few candidates who seem, at least on the surface, to have a better claim. One name that crops up again and again is that of Columba – or Columcille – the saint of Iona. Now, although he was a man of the cloth, Columba was a wheeler-dealer and you can make out a good case for him beginning to pull the Scots and the Picts together, hundreds of years before the man who always gets the credit – Kenneth MacAlpin.

Detractors will tell you that Columba was an upstart Irish prince, a chancer who left us with an identity crisis.

Columba will have advocates but I imagine, in the south-west, folk would make a strong case for St Ninian (*floruit c.* AD 400), the first missionary to Scotland whose name is known. Also I've a feeling you would gather a good few votes for the saintly Margaret, wife of Malcolm Canmore. Mungo might have a shout and maybe Patrick could re-establish a Scottish–Irish connection.

Vince Dougal
The Strip, Peel Glen, Ullapool

Then again, if you were simply having a wee laugh, you might opt for St Martha, patron saint of dieticians, or St John of God, patron saint of heart patients. However, that perhaps is just a little too close to home — Ed.

Jewels in the Crown

In its long history Scotland has surely accumulated many beautiful and valuable artefacts. What is generally considered to be Scotland's greatest national treasure?

Lars Thistlethwaite
Rocky Bottom, Emmerslade, Midlothian

I have absolutely no doubt that Scotland's greatest treasure is Edinburgh Castle standing resplendently on its volcanic rock, where the pageant of Scottish history has been enacted and which has witnessed the heart of this nation in moments of triumph and despair. Nowhere in this fair land is there such a noble prospect. You can keep your Burns country and your Callanish Standing Stones, your St

Kilda and your Glencoe. Edinburgh's glory, its castle, stands aboon them all.

Felix Snark
MSP for the Posh Parts of Edinburgh,
The Upturned Boats, by Holyrood

Nae question but that our two greatest national treasures huv tae be Lulu and wee Jimmy Krankie. They both make you proud to be Scots. By the way, they are both wee brammers – at least to my discerning eye. And, just in case, because I'm admiring wee Jimmy, you reckon I fancy him, Ah huv tae tell you that wee Jimmy is a wumman – honest tae God. And I'm no' that way inclined. I was going tae include Alex McLeish, the late lamented Rangers boss, 'cause my wee boy telt me tae but Ah've never trusted carrot-tops.

Ella Rothesay, Mrs
Stall 4, 'Neath the Brig, Paddy's Market, Saltmarket, Glasgow

The question quite honestly does not have to be asked. If you wish to see the real Scotland, this land's greatest treasure, you must visit the Mearns with its rolling farmland reaching up to the mountains, its lazy rivers, its sailing cloud-shapes over the Howe, its couthy, occasionally carnaptious, people, its marvellous coos. From Drumlithie to Forfar, the heart of ancient Pictland remains largely unchanged and unspoiled by the modern world – apart, of course, from the infernal A94. It is a russet, fruitful landscape which has inspired poetry, art and hard work. It has encouraged good, honest folk to draw the harvests from the earth as year drifts into year and century into century.

Uist Grass-Seed Gibson
Oootermuckery, by Laurencekirk, Kincardineshire

I would like to nominate my mother, Madge Mackintosh, as Scotland's greatest national treasure. Despite a whole series of domestic tragedies and mysterious absences from home, she brought me up to work hard and respect other people. Her involvement with the Bridgeton bullion robbery of 1998, she says, was a complete set-up and the twenty-year sentence an injustice. She says she only made the corned beef sandwiches for the gang. Well, she's a treasure to me, anyway. If me mother is disqualified, then I would like to nominate the Barras Market or Dougie Donnelly or Clydebank Football Club or . . .

Mij Snowhite
The New Age Encampment, Aberfoyle, Stirlingshire

Brass Monkeys

With global warming, we might expect exceptionally cold winters to end. Before we do, can anyone tell me what is regarded as Scotland's worst winter and just how severe were conditions?

Gale Forrest
Bendigo, Australia

Gale, our most severe winter is a matter of some debate simply because, statistics apart, the severity of the weather – whether it be storms, floods, snow or ice – is very much in the eye of the beholder.

I would like to nominate 1963 simply because it was within my own lifetime and the snowfall was among the heaviest in living memory, particularly in January and February of that year. The entire country was blanketed by huge drifts. I was in the Borders where the River Tweed froze solid. Helicopters were used to bring pregnant mothers from rural districts to hospitals in the cities. If I remember correctly, this became known as Operation Stork. Clever, eh? Drifts up to twenty-feet deep were commonplace. Villages were cut off for days, trains badly affected and snow cornices above the Edinburgh–Carlisle rail line in Roxburghshire had to be blown up with dynamite to prevent them collapsing on passing trains.

I'm told that the severity of winters in Central Scotland at least is often judged by how extensively Loch Lomond is frozen. Well, in 1963 sightseers were able to walk out and around the *Maid of the Loch*, frozen into her berth at Balloch Pier. My greatest regret that winter was that for weeks football matches were cancelled.

Bill Winterson
Elie, Fife

It is always interesting when people assume that severe winter weather is the direct result of changing climatic conditions. To look at the confident weather forecasters on television, one would think that they had all the answers. Mr Winterson drew attention to the winter of 1963 which, I would argue, is a classic example of bad weather caused by seismic disturbances deep within the earth. The actual mechanics of this process are complex for the man or woman in the street to grasp but British seismo-meteorologists believe that ghost tremors, reaching upwards into the atmosphere from the location of earth shocks, prevent normal reheating of the earth's atmosphere following a potentially short-lived cold snap. As a result, the affected area becomes sealed into a deep freeze.

Prof. Cyrus Magma
The Locked Ward, Sule Skerry, Shetland

There are many candidates for the worst Scottish winter. You might want to look at 1795 or 1694, certainly 1895 would come into the reckoning. My own favourite goes back a long, long way to 1301 when there was what can only be described as a national disaster.

The historian Hector Boece described how conditions became so severe that beer froze into lumps and was sold by the pound. An interesting concept which conjures up images of grown Scotsmen sooking their ale lumps. Just by way of contrast, there have been signs of global warming for decades. In 1983, the mildest winter for many years, wild birds got themselves into a real state. Thrushes and blackbirds began building their nests in the middle of January. It is now generally accepted that birds are nesting more than two weeks earlier than they did thirty years ago.

Macaskill Fish
Institute of Interesting Weather Stories, Penge, Greater London

3

Patter and pelters

If it Wisnae for the Wallies . . .

Why has that great international Clydeside comedian Billy Connolly apparently become a figure of hate for the Scottish press? Is it simply because of his overuse of the F-word?

Joe Kerr
Leading Midshipman, HMS *Hilarius*, beneath the North Pole

There is a section of the Scottish public who believe that the use of the F-word, now commonplace on television, brought about Billy Connolly's partial fall from grace. There is no doubt his sketches have become increasingly sprinkled with curses but, in reality, this was only a small factor in this strange falling-out – the cause was rooted deep in the culture of Scotland.

Billy Connolly made a basic mistake. For years, he had harvested the goodwill of the Scottish people with his brilliant observational skills and earthy shipyard humour. He was in tune with the way that people felt and thought . . . and then he blew it. In the simplest terms, he got 'bigsy' and that, in the view of most Scots, is unforgivable.

It seems that Billy was swept away by his success and there is nothing the Scottish people and their Rottweiler press love to hate more than someone who has made the big time and flaunts their celebrity in the faces of their fellow Caledonians by hob-nobbing with junior royalty and second-rate television and movie stars. More than that, Billy seemed to enjoy the experience and openly revelled in his new status. Rightly or wrongly, people believed that he had abandoned his working-class roots. Once again this was seen as unforgivable. In a tight-knit community like Scotland, where everyone is watching their neighbours, there is no escape from the spotlight. When you raise your head above the parapet, prepare to have it shot off!

There is still an element in Scottish society that resents success, seeing it as a selfish adventure. Those who have got above themselves often leave family, friends and simple truths trailing in their wake. The sense of community and sharing which they might once have espoused is abandoned in the rush to material success.

Of course, Billy probably couldn't give a toss for what any of us think and he definitely went one better than most of the bigsy folk – he bought himself a fucking castle! I'm still awaiting the dinner invite.

Elphinstone Turf
Senior Shop Steward, Brannigan's Bolt Factory, Scotstoun Road, Glasgow

Billy Connolly remains one of the most talented stand-up comedians produced in Scotland in the past half-century, a simply inspired bystander/recorder of the Scots and the world at large at work and play. I think certain sections of the media and some of his more middle-class fans turned against the Big Yin because he crossed the fine line between self-confidence and overconfidence. He fell victim to a Scottish mindset which demands that people do not get ideas above their station. In a sense he betrayed his Scottishness.

Probably even more importantly, Mr Connolly is quite clearly comfortable with who he is – he feels no embarrassment at success, no guilt about being a celebrity. That just won't do, will it?

Walter Witman
Crannog 42, Lock Eck, Argyll

Sweets for my Sweet

Scotland's record of dental hygiene, particularly among young children, has been one of the worst in the world. Why do Scots seem to have such a sweet tooth compared with the rest of the world?

Bonbon Lefevre
Rue de Chocolat, Dieppe, France

'Ally Bally, Ally Bally Be . . .' If you recognise the opening line from the song about Coltart's Candy, then you are probably of the generation who remember the sweetie shop on the corner with the long rows of bottles filled with unspeakable delights such as pan drops, soor plooms, barley sugars and aniseed balls. We do love our sweeties in Scotland and this obsession can be dated to the first importation of sugar from the West Indies in the 1680s, after which sugar refineries sprang up in Greenock, Glasgow and Dundee.

It is now pretty well established that too much sugar can wreak havoc with your tooth enamel. Yet you'll still find that, at the cinema, the vast majority of Scots still prefer tubs of sweet popcorn to the salty variety and, on the move, Scottish drivers devour far more sweeties than their English counterparts.

However, the fact that we are so slow on the uptake about the effects too much sugar has not just on our teeth but on our bodies is understandable. It isn't so many years since the older generation were actively encouraging children to take 'boilings' because they were actually good for you, warding off colds etc. It may take a few generations yet before this mindset is altered. Meantime a large market for old-fashioned sweetie-shop delights has now emerged on the internet. You can't win, can you?

Phil McCavitty
Tuath Da Danaan, Aggregate Road, Arbroath

The sweet tooth is indeed an unusually Scottish characteristic, I think. Other countries tend to specialise in a particular variety of sweet – like the Belgians with their chocolates – but, here in Scotland, we attack the whole range of sweets from deep-fried chocolate bars, through jelly beans to the classic coconut snowball with a few thousand other 'delicacies' in between.

Tablet and fudge are still widely made in Scotland although one American visitor recently described our home-made tablet, produced from a formula handed down to us by Bonnie Prince Charlie's cook, as a 'cholesterol bomb'. If he thought it was bad for his heart, wait until his teeth start dropping out.

My own favourite sweet would have to be the giant aniseed ball, round, red, shiny, hard as iron and with an explosive core that can blow your mind. Its sheer bulk should also have necessitated an attached explanatory leaflet illustrating how to apply the Heimlich Manoeuvre to a choking devotee. That indeed sums up one of the problems with sweets in the twenty-first century. There is a great demand for everything to be healthy and nutritious, each sweet must comply with the strictures of the health and safety regulations. A new generation of sweets is emerging but I fear that never again will we have the joy of entering the sweetie shop, pushing our pennies with grubby fingers across the glass counter and demanding, 'A quarter of dolly mixtures.'

Mrs Candy Ball
Sweetheart Road, Hawick, Borders

The Scottish enjoyment of sweets should not be allowed to disguise the heinous exploitation of thousands of African slaves in the Caribbean sugar plantations, a crime which brought prosperity to Glasgow and misery to many others. Incidentally, I've always felt that Scots have been improperly made to feel guilty about their sweet tooth. It is known that all mammals enjoy sweetness and, if, as we're told, fewer mothers now breastfeed, then this would explain a craving amongst that generation of youngsters. Then again, it might just be comfort eating in our unpredictable climate.

Comrade Dan McLean
Mick McGahey House, Clartyhole Mews, Dumbarton

Seeing is Believing

People in Scotland insist that the Brahan Seer was a prophet who ranks up alongside Ezekiel and Nostradamus. Is this not just another example of the 'Wha's like us?' syndrome?

Ann Tissipate (née Forsyte)
Rue Fourneau, Marseille, France

The Brahan Seer has indeed been described as Scotland's very own Nostradamus (incidentally, he was almost a contemporary of the French soothsayer) gazing into the future and producing riddles and images which can be interpreted as inspired predictions or lucky leaps of imagination depending on your inclination.

His 'ability' was generally known in Scotland as 'second sight', that is seeing in a vision events before they take place. Very often this took the form of a prevision of death or a symbol of that event – a shroud, a candle or a corpse. People who have studied the three-centuries'-old predictions of the Brahan Seer, Coinneach Mackenzie, have been impressed by his big successes. Among events he is said to have predicted are the Highland Clearances and the discovery of North Sea oil.

But, for me, it is on inconsequential happenings that his ability should be judged. Gazing through a hole in a small black-bluish river stone the Brahan Seer came up with some cracking predictions. For example, 'When five spires should rise in Strathpeffer, a ship will sail over the village and anchor to them.' This all sounded like a load of hooey until, in the 1850s, an Episcopal church with an impressive spire was built in the town bringing the total number of spires to five. Shortly after World War One, it seems, a small airship was a feature of the Strathpeffer Games and, having dropped a grapnel in preparation for landing, it became entangled in one of the spires, anchoring the airship.

To me at least, this wee prediction compares very favourably with the rather vague and generalised sort of declarations which we usually get from the likes of Nostradamus. We should have no embarrassment about or reluctance to trumpet our seers. They come from an important Celtic tradition where the seer had a vital role to play in the organisation of the community. More recently, before the advent of the telephone, computers and the internet, the seer might be asked to check out the fortunes of family members who had emigrated.

Lawrence Legend
The Hovel, Killiecrankie, Perthshire

If you want more recent confirmation of the ability of Highlanders to see into the future, you can simply consult the predictions of the late Swein MacDonald who hailed from Ross and Cromarty. In the second half of the twentieth century, he was the most famous of contemporary Highland seers. MacDonald had the *Braer* oil tanker grounding in Shetland, the Falklands War and the divorce of Charles and Diana on his CV. A practical Highlander, MacDonald made a living giving his view of proposed big business deals to Far East executives.

In an interview in 1998, Swein explained that his predictions weren't always spot on. He said that the images were in his mind's eye, flashing past just like on television. But he was also the first to admit that he didn't always understand what he was seeing with his third eye. I know what he means – I get the same effect from three pints of Guinness. Asked why he hadn't avoided the misfortunes which had strewn his own life's path, MacDonald said, 'I get warnings but I'm a thrawn old devil and I won't listen to them.'

In this new age when everyone and their brother seems to be reading Tarot cards, toying with I Ching, offering spiritual guidance or gazing meaningfully into a crystal ball, the likes of Swein are the real McCoy.

Thomas Doubting
The Mercat Cross, Brechin, Angus

Belt It Out

The Great Scottish Anthem Debate – is there a stirring ancient Caledonian alternative to the more modern musical pretenders or are we stuck forever and a day with the customary dirges and the usual heedorum-hoderum-ism?

Ben Digit
Romford Takeaway Foods, The Kasbah, Ealing Broadway, London

Since I was knee-high to a sporran people, in Scotland at least, seem to have been arguing about Scotland's anthem. 'Scotland the Brave' is a jaunty celebration of tartan mania, 'Flower of Scotland' is an anthem more suitable for a Scottish Remembrance Day and 'Scots Wha Hae' is unquestionably a call to arms.

Surely it is not beyond the wit of the Scots who turn out fine musicians, artists, lyricists, poets, singers to come up with something which will celebrate the wonderful gift of Scottishness instead of bemoaning previous injustices and threatening violence to all and sundry who cross our path, particularly if they happen to be English. I would suggest a fairly up-tempo version of 'Loch Lomond', a song which Donnie Munro and Runrig used to perform with such obvious gusto. And frankly, after a glass or two of the bendy juice, I have found that the thumping base line in The Proclaimers' 'Five Hundred Miles' fair gets the sap rising.

Oh, yes, of course, there is a medieval alternative – the melody 'Hey Tutti Tatti' was sung by the Scots army on its way to Bannockburn according to some of the old chroniclers.

Melody Staffa
Bolton Path, Nairn

Really, I don't see what the problem is with this anthem business. It's quite clear that, as a nation, we will never settle on a choice that is going to make everyone happy. This is just another reflection of the fact that, although we are a small place, we are also a mixed-up, mongrel nation and a tune that might suit someone from Kyle of Lochalsh can seem totally alien to someone from Kelso. As a third generation Italian-Scot, I now feel entitled to join this debate and appeal for some common sense.

During the 2006 World Cup, the answer to all this soul-searching jumped out at us from the television screens. Adopt an anthem – then we'll never tire of the same old monotonous dirge. There would be a new lament every year for us to criticise and then unceremoniously abandon. Just at this moment, with Scotland being overrun by new workers from Eastern Europe, the Polish anthem seems appropriate. I thought that the anthems of Togo and Paraguay could also be 'borrowed' on a temporary basis since they are so undistinguished that they make 'Flower of Scotland' seem like a genuine cry from the heart.

And why shouldn't we make a start with the national anthem of South Korea? Their team was managed in the last World Cup by that Govanite manqué, Dick Advocaat, and I'm told by the usual unreliable sources that their anthem used to be sung to the tune of 'Auld Lang Syne'. In actual fact, if you have a listen to the current South Korean melody, it is vaguely Rubovian with a touch of the Moody and Sankey. Maybe the Scottish connection hasn't been completely lost.

Suru Nagpal-Frapanelli
Seven Hills of Rome, 14 Canal Street, Wishaw

Yo-Ho-Ho

I understand that the Celtic tribe which gave Scotland her name was really just a bunch of Irish pirates and that strictly speaking we should be the painted people and living in Pictland.

Thatcher Scold
The Bothy, Mains of Bogskelpet, by Inverurie

It's hardly in dispute these days – the people who crossed from Ulster to Argyll in the first centuries of the Christian era were the Scotti, an Irish tribe of colonisers who gave their name to Scotland. Latin writers referred to the inhabitants of Ireland as Scotti and to Ireland itself as Scotia.

To the Roman mind, everyone outwith their influence was a barbarian. Pirate was a description in the same category and this was how the Romans described the Scotti. Although the wild Celtic tribes were indeed not averse to a bit of sea raiding, pirate was just another insult hurled at an ancient people beyond the sway of Rome.

Had the Scots, who brought their own language, the so-called 'Q' version of Gaelic, not anchored themselves in the west and eventually after generations of warfare assimilated the remains of the Pictish nation either by conquest or osmosis, then the northern territory which we now occupy might indeed just as easily have been called Pictland. Although it is important to point out that the Picti, or the Caledonii as they are sometimes described, may simply have been a loose confederation of tribes.

However, they were a cultured, sophisticated people who, I would contend, would have made a better fist of getting the nation organised than the wild Scots. In essence, Mr Scold has the situation correctly. We live in a land which was occupied and conquered by outsiders, foreigners, the Scots of Dalriada, centuries before our English cousins south of the Border started to noise us up and sought to put us under their sway. The Picts are the true 'fathers' of our nation.

Pete Medden
14 Chariot Road, Back o' Bennachie, Aberdeenshire

As usual Peter the Pict has his head in the clouds. The Picts were never a nation and never, it would seem, a cultural unity although their art and their ogham script seem to suggest some sort of shared experience. He hits the correct note when he mentions the possibility that they were merely an unconsolidated group of tribes. My guess is that they were not so ambitious or politically adept as the Scots of Dalriada and this was their downfall. We should also remember that the man who, by all common sense, should be Scotland's patron saint, Columba, sprang from the seed bed of Ulster before settling in Dalriadic Iona.

What is much more interesting is the mythic or legendary history of Scotland. The earliest Scots historians, after much poring over dusty tomes and several glasses of heather ale, managed to track a history for the Scots which takes us back to Greece and Egypt. Gathelus, a bit of a Greek rough boy, fled to Egypt, married Scota, the daughter of the pharaoh who oppressed the Israelites and, when the famous plagues hit town, he sailed off into the sunset where he set up camp first of all in Portugal (the port of Gathelus), then moved on to Galicia. By this time, the tribe were known as the Scots in honour of his wife. From there Gathelus sent his sons to achieve a foothold in Ireland which they had spotted from the top of a rather tall tower in northern Spain.

With adventuring in their blood, it was only a matter

of time before they crossed to the wild country that was eventually to bear their name.

Now, this may be described as the mythical history of the Scots but the story of Scota and her adventures has a very authentic ring. Don't you think so?

Johnno Lorne
Roonra Ben, Dalnaspidal, Perthshire

Fore Play

Why does Scotland insist on calling itself 'The Home of Golf'? Surely golf like bagpipes and haggis developed much earlier elsewhere. What is it about you Scots that you have to grab credit for everything?

Boris Shanker
Rue de Vieux Tom Morris, Bruxelles, Belgium

I too have often wondered why we seem so determined to grab all the glory as the Mecca of golf. It is patently clear that we did not invent the game and that the sport of golf grew organically. Admittedly, there is a much-quoted edict from the Scottish Parliament in 1457 ordering that 'futeball and golf be utterly cryit doon and nocht usit'. The people were ordered to take up archery which was seen as a much more profitable pastime in such warlike times. However, the game's pedigree on the world stage is much more ancient and relatively easy to trace.

We find the Romans having a golf-style knockabout in a game called *paganica* which, as far as can be established, involved hitting a feather-stuffed ball with some form of club. Just as the British sports of the nineteenth century were carried throughout the old Empire, it seems distinctly possible that golf-mad legionaries brought this rustic sport to northern Europe. In medieval England, there was a jolly olde sport called *cambuca* which was a ball and club game and had similarities to a French variant called *jeu de mail*. We probably have to concede that the word golf comes from the Dutch but that particular game was apparently a croquet-style indoor event, normally played in a barn, and involved the use of only one club. Odd folk those flatlanders . . .

What we can claim, despite a surprising absence of a history prior to the edict of 1457, is that it was in Scotland that the sport of golf flourished and was nurtured and, as a result, Scotland could, indeed, with all the afore-mentioned provisos, be called the Home of Golf. After all, the Honourable Company at Muirfield in East Lothian drew up the first written rules known to the game (thirteen in all) in 1744, the Royal and Ancient at St Andrews was formed ten years later and the first recorded inter-club golf match between the Edinburgh Burgess Golfing Society and Bruntsfield Links Golf Club took place in 1818. I rest my case.

Cilla Green
National Museum of Putting,
Decent Drive, Muirfield, East Lothian

Over the years I have collected little snippets which, I believe, confirm Scotland's claim to be the Home of Golf. For example, in 1504 a golf challenge match between James IV and the Earl of Bothwell took place – the result is unrecorded, suggesting a royal defeat. Duncan Forbes, the eighteenth-century Lord President of the Court of Session, wrote to friends during the 1745 Jacobite Uprising complaining that he couldn't have his customary game of golf at Musselburgh because of the troubles. And Mary, Queen of Scots, fighting back the tears no doubt, had a round of golf within a few hours of the death of Darnley. For me, it has been the introduction of imaginative eccentricity to the game which is the most telling confirmation of the sport as Scotland's own. Back in the early days, Andrew McKellar of Edinburgh loved the game so much he persuaded friends to hold lanterns so that he could play the short holes at Bruntsfield Links by night.

With such a pedigree who daur meddle with our golfing inheritance?

Mattie Niblick
The 19th Green Cocktail Bar,
Palm Springs Memorial Course, Fetlar, Shetland

Back to Scandinavia

Should the Northern Isles be set adrift and returned to the control of Norway and thus save Scotland a fortune in transport subsidies?

Felix Snark
MSP for the Posh Parts of Edinburgh,
The Upturned Boats, by Holyrood

It drives me mad to think how much residents of Central Scotland are expected to pay through their taxes to keep a crew of teuchters, English immigrants, drop-outs and mushroom chompers happy in the western Highlands and Islands.

Now that's bad enough but at least these places from Cape Wrath to Campbeltown are definitively part of Scotland – not so those weird locations which TV weather folk call the Northern Isles, Orkney and Shetland. Why should we be paying to preserve links between Scotland and these remote backwaters where the folk don't even consider themselves Scots?

I'm told that both Orkney and Shetland councils have vast reserve funds, gathered over the past decades from the involvement in North Sea oil and carefully locked away for a rainy day. Well, that rainy day may be nearer than they think. Why don't these councils dig into their bulging pooches to pay for ferry and air links instead of asking folk in the cities to fork out on their behalf?

Five and half centuries ago the islands were part of the kingdom of Denmark when they were pledged by the Danish king as a dowry for his daughter Margaret when she married James III, King of Scots. In other words, the Danish king got rid of some territory of questionable value. Orkney was reckoned to be worth 50,000 florins and Shetland a mere but very realistic 8,000 florins. In a sense, you can't blame the ordinary Shetlanders and Orcadians – they were pawns in this political game and probably never wanted to be Scots in the first place. They just woke up one morning and found they were Scottish. For many people south of Gretna, that is simply a nightmare.

So let's cast the Northern Islanders adrift again. They don't want to be Scottish and, on rejoining Scandinavia, they would soon get used to paying £10 for a pint of lager and supporting Brann Bergen which frankly sounds more like a laxative than a football team.

Billy Bottomley
The Manse, Truro Road, Dalmellington, Ayrshire

What an offensive piece of nonsense you printed in your May edition from Mr Bottomley of Dalmellington. He completely ignores the powerful links between Orkney and Shetland and

Scotland which have been nurtured over the years and which were in existence long before the islands were absorbed through treaty. In the world wars of the twentieth century, islanders made the ultimate sacrifice for their country in the services. The island groups have, over the centuries, sent their young folk south to become doctors, lawyers and politicians and to influence the shaping of Britain in a myriad of ways. They helped build the British Empire. For example, at one time, 70 per cent of the employees of the Hudson's Bay Company were Orcadians.

If the people of these islands chose to maintain an independence of spirit within the United Kingdom that recognises their Scandinavian heritage, then that can surely be nothing but a good thing. Do we want a homogenous, standardised nation without character and personality where every region is very similar to its neighbour, without any distinctive heritage? This is happening in various parts of the United Kingdom – it makes people easier to control. But God forbid that the number crunchers get their way. To keep the nation spiritually alive, sense of community in the more remote corners must be fostered, nurtured and, when necessary, subsidised. Scotland has surely already learned the hard lessons of allowing the land to empty.

In the same way that the Gaelic peoples of the Highlands can celebrate their Irish/Celtic roots and be encouraged in that tradition by government, so must the interest in the Scandinavian roots of Orkney and Shetland be accepted and encouraged without allowing blind, Central-Scotland prejudice to creep into the equation.

We are a mongrel nation, Scotland. And a vital component in that wonderful mix is the Scandinavian

heritage found not only in the Northern Isles but throughout the land.

Simeon Seetay
Peel o' Bells, Back Road, Unst, Shetland

Personally, you can cast us adrift any time you like. Shetland
and Orkney have no need to be associated with the narrow,
navel-gazing negativity that characterises Scottish society.
But, be warned, we will be keeping all our oil revenues – and
the new Atlantic reserves of oil.

Theorolf Pick
The Cliff Edge, Outertoon, Orkney

Our Haunted Hills

*Scotland's castles seem to be overcrowded with ghosts and
supernatural activity but are there any records of ghosts on the
Scottish mountains?*

Addie Gimpy
Fit o' the Brae, Glen Lyon, Perthshire

Ghosts are an important element in the Scottish tourist
industry and it's a strange castle indeed that does not have
legends of headless pipers, strangled chambermaids or balmy
butlers who return nightly to haunt and harass the living.
Scottish towns and, in particular, one of the most ghostly cities
in Europe, Edinburgh, have umpteen legends of hauntings.
As you might expect, the Old Town is especially rich in them
– ghost tours thrive on the stories of Warlock Weir and a
frightening team of spectres who patrol the echoing closes
and wynds. But I would argue that it is in the Scottish hills

and glens that the most fascinating ghost stories are to be found.

Strange balls of lightning or *gealbhain* have been known in the Highlands for hundreds of years, appearing completely out of the blue and vanishing after a brief, if spectacular, 'performance'. The area around Lochs Tay and Rannoch seem particularly favoured with fiery globes seen rising from the water and skipping across the surface. Apparitions of Highlanders have been seen at a variety of locations – including Glencoe near the site of the infamous massacre of 1692. But it is not just ghosts in human form that find a home in the Highlands.

Old buildings in the hills have a very special atmosphere which, even if they afford shelter from the storm, don't always encourage the walker to spend a night within their walls. Veteran climber Hamish MacInnes told of how two members of a mountain rescue team walking in the Glen Affric area saw a cottage on the verge of a loch where no cottage, as far as is known, has ever existed. Within a short time it disappeared. Astonishingly they discovered that the 'ghost cottage' had been seen before.

Why shouldn't our hills be good locations for encountering supernatural phenomena? If ghosts, as we believe, are the spirits of the unhappy deceased locked into their last corporeal surroundings, then the mountains of Scotland, so rich in dramatic, bloodthirsty and romantic history, must inevitably have a story to tell.

Sally Spectre
The Deep, Dark Wood, near Ruchazie, Glasgow

Without a shadow of a doubt, the most interesting and enduring ghostly legend of the Scottish mountains is that of the *Fear Laith Mor* – the Big Grey Man – of Ben Macdhui. This odd phenomenon was reported for the first time in 1925 by an eminent London professor. He was descending alone from the summit of Ben Macdhui when he heard crunching footsteps in the snow – and they were not his own. Whoever was following him appeared to have a huge stride. It is merely an apocryphal addendum to this story that, when asked what steps he took on discovering he was being followed by a spectre, the professor replied, 'Bloody big ones!'

Other climbers claim to have seen a giant figure, ten feet tall, clambering from the Lairg Ghru towards the summit cairn. Interestingly, while some people claim to have seen the Big Grey Man, others in the same group of climbers may have seen nothing.

There is also a strange inhabitant of the Loch Ness area. The apparition is known to the Highlanders as the Old Man of Inverfarigaig but is more often heard than seen. His screaming echoes among the leafless trees fringing the lochside, particularly during winter storms. Cynical observers suggest that this may be nothing more than an unusual effect of the wind in the trees – others, perhaps wisely, reserve judgement.

The effect of wind on the snow this time has also been one of the many explanations of the Big Grey Man. He has also been explained away as the shadow of a cloud passing across the mountain face.

Sanjeev Munro
Sky Television Call Centre, Bangalore, India

There seems little doubt that very strange things happen in Scotland's mountains and glens. For more than just safety reasons, it is best to take a companion with you into the high places! — Ed.

Two Peas in a Pod?

Is it possible to tell an Englishman and a Scotsman apart? Is there actually any real difference between the species? And does it matter?

Pancho Systematico

International House, Longniddry, East Lothian

Several times in recent years, the idea that the Scots and the English are somehow different, that they constitute separate ethnic groupings within this sceptred isle, has been tested at industrial tribunals where unfair treatment has been claimed due to nationality. The two most interesting cases that come to mind occurred within three weeks of each other in 1997 when four air stewardesses claimed they had dropped to the bottom of a seniority list when they moved from the Scottish Highlands Division of BA to worldwide services because they were Scottish. And a deputy chief constable in Lothian and Borders Police argued that he had been passed over by the Northern Joint Police Board for promotion because he was English. The tribunal in the case of the stewardesses decided that there is no ethnic difference between the Scots and the English while the police case tribunal concluded that there was. Confusion reigns.

William Wallace (alias Mel Gibson) chanted in *Braveheart*, 'They may take away oor lives but they will never take away oor fr-*e-e-e-e*-dom.' That kind of suggests that the film-makers at least believed that the Scots were fighting to retain some sort of distinct identity. The history books tell the same story. Today, north of the Border, there is a strong perception that the people of England have somehow mislaid whatever identity and ethnicity they may have had and that they have become merely an American sub-culture. As one distinguished Scottish advocate was heard to say at the action against the Northern Police Board, 'My submission is that Rastafarians seem to have more of an argument for being an ethnic group than Englishmen.'

For that reason, we pity our English cousins who only ever seem to unite with one voice when 1966 is mentioned. National identity is not something to be ashamed of as long as it shows itself in positive, cheerful ways. We are fortunate here in Scotland to still have an acute sense of who we are. Long may that continue.

Peter Patullo
Keeper of the Records, Hogganfield Loch Model Yacht Owners Association, The Boathouse, Stepps, Glasgow

Whenever this topic is raised, the easy solution for me is simply to quote Lord Simon of Glaisdale speaking at an appeal case in London in 1971. It shows very succinctly that history quite simply makes the Scots and English different. He declared:

> The Scots are a nation because of Bannockburn and Flodden, Culloden and the pipes at Lucknow; because of Jenny Geddes and Flora MacDonald, because of frugal living and respect for learning, because of Robert Burns and Sir Walter Scott. So, too, the English are a nation – because Norman, Angevin and Tudor monarchs forged them together, because their land is mostly sea girt, because of the common law and of gifts for poetry and parliamentary government . . .

Sir Albert Dodsley
Hubris Hall, Skelsmorsdale, Lancashire

The all-British developments of the past 100 years – including the creation of the welfare state, the world war against fascism, the move towards closer links with Europe – have, through shared experience, erased differences and left a homogenous British society. For example, the supposedly bitter hatred of England and all things English exhibited amongst Scotland's football supporters? It's a myth. I would argue that when you pin those fans down individually (some would say that's the best thing for 'em), remove them from the tribal setting of the terracings, the vast majority will tell you that they feel no real animosity towards England or the English.

The fact is that the English now happily celebrate Hogmanay and the birthday of Robbie the Bard and the news that morris dancing is growing in popularity in places like Bellshill and Clydebank would seem to suggest that we will, despite minor hiccups like the Scottish Parliament, soon be one nation under God – or the Church of England.

Sam Goldworthy
Author of *Are We Really the Peepel? – A Study of Scots Jingoism*, Wimbledon, London

Isn't it absurd to suggest that an Act of Parliament, the 1707 Act of Union, bringing two nations together as one should have been the beginning of the end of the sense of Scottishness, something which so many Scots clearly still feel? Thankfully, for most people this is not a sour, anti-English stance but simply a pride in being Scottish – knowing, or sensing, a little about our dark and marvellous history.

Defining a Scot in the modern world, however, is proving to be difficult. A Scottish accent and four Scottish grandparents is a help. Some might argue that mere residence in the country is sufficient to entitle you to call yourself a Scot. I would say that someone who sells off their single end in Chelsea and buys a Scottish estate with the intention of lording it for a wee while and then moving on is not entitled to call themselves a Scot.

On the other hand, incomers who show an understanding of and a willingness to identify with our traditions and our culture, in the broadest sense, would have earned the coveted label of 'Scot'.

At the end of the day we are all human beings. Perhaps eventually governments will force the Scots, Irish, Welsh – and English – into intellectual, social and political conformity – perhaps. But in the meantime – *Vive la différence!*

Axel Greece
Mechanics Shop, The Bus Garage, Aberfeldy, Perthshire

Yeah, you can tell the difference – the Scot is wearing the 'See You, Jimmy' hat and the daft grin and the Englishman is wearing a scowl.

Bonner Bridge
The Underpass, Cowcaddens, Glasgow

The most important point in this debate is that a Scot doesn't need to be told he or she is Scottish. Being Scottish is not about waving flags, wearing Highland dress and supporting the underdog, it is about what you feel in your heart — Ed.

Take the Floor!

On holiday in Scotland, we were invited to a night of country dancing at Auchenblane House. We found the whole evening very staid and the dancing very stuffy. Is Scottish country dancing always so formal?

Dunty Glennan
The Willows, Riperatawahuwaikiki Road,
Wellington, New Zealand

It's a great pity that Dunty saw only one side of the wonderful pastime of Scottish country dancing during her visit. She clearly encountered the 'county set' at play and these folk – petty nobility and upper-middle-class snobs, privately educated (often in England), frequently with a double-barrel name – are not at all representative of Scottish country dancing, or Scotland for that matter.

There is another world of wildly energetic Scottish country dancing among young people – and old – who are proud to be Scots without necessarily getting togged up in tartanry, who laugh in the face of formality and thoroughly enjoy themselves, even if, in the confusion, men occasionally end up dancing with men, women with women.

You'll find this everywhere from city clubs to village halls, and the enthusiasm with which these folk dance the dances is something which visitors to Scotland from all over, who are privileged enough to witness or participate in, never forget. The kilt is optional, the smile compulsory. Scottish country dance is a product of the Highland culture of ordinary folk expressing itself in wonderful vitality. It is a world away from the stuffed-shirt prancing of the self-styled nobs found in country houses and the pricey hotel extravaganzas laid on for the benefit of tourists.

Eva Tostepp
Balfron Braes, Kinnoul, Perthshire

Delightful though it was to see Eva Tostepp gliding to the defence of Scottish county dancing in its egalitarian setting I fear when she has gone badly off-track if she thinks that Scottish country dancing has its origins in the Highlands. Nothing could be further from the truth.

There's no doubt that social dancing among ordinary people was commonplace in medieval Scotland. In the early 1400s, for example, regular fairs and markets, weddings, even funerals provided a chance for lads and lassies to indulge in what seems to have been the most popular dance – the Salmon – which apparently consisted of active leaps like those of the fish from which it takes its name. And we thought pogoing punks were something new?

But the brief reign of Mary, Queen of Scots in the 1500s was an Indian summer for dancing in Scotland. For most of the 1600s 'social dancing' was condemned by the Kirk as sinful. Reformers surely had in mind the more modern maxim that dancing is only a perpendicular expression of a horizontal desire. For example, some Elgin girls committed a serious offence in dancing with a piper in 1619 and in 1649 'promiscuous dancing', nothing more salacious than men dancing with women, was banned by the Kirk.

It was in the early eighteenth century that a more tolerant attitude to what dance scholars Joan and Thomas Flett have called 'the lighter pleasure' began to be seen and social dancing regained its popularity. There is much speculation about the re-emergence of the Scottish dance but the evidence suggests that it was a lowland development which only reached the more remote parts of the Highlands and Orkney between 1850 and 1890.

Jack Gilchrist
Swing Your Partner Medieval Dance Club, Rothesay

Perhaps the most interesting aspect of the debate about Scottish country dance relates to its origins – and prepare for a stunning, some would say 'daft', suggestion – Scottish country dancing originated in England. The generally accepted view, believe it or not, is that the country dance which appeared in Scotland around 1700 was of English origin, bearing similarities to the dances found south of the Border. I think this is most unlikely. Does it not make much more sense that the traditional Scottish country dance, the 'longways progressive' of the Middle Ages, simply went underground during the cheerless years of the seventeenth century and resurfaced when the social atmosphere was a bit less frigid?

Sho-be Reppard
The Nae Breeks Scottish Dance Club, Accra, Ghana

Beyond Duntocher

Has anyone any theories as to why the Roman Empire apparently called a halt to its headlong expansionism when they reached Central Scotland?

Anthony Mark
The Forum Public House, Eagle Grove, Govan

The failure of the Romans to make any genuine impact in Scotland beyond the Highland line has been the source of discussion and academic debate for many years.

The received wisdom suggests that the Highlands, as wild and barbarous a land as the legions of the Empire had encountered, was simply regarded as not worth the effort and cost of policing or colonising.

But I have my own theory about why they stopped at the

line of the Antonine Wall, at least at its western extremity. What could the legions have found that made them think twice about regular sorties into the Arrochar Alps and beyond? Cannibals – that's what! The history books tell us that there was a tribe on the northern banks of the Clyde, in the vicinity of Loch Lomond and the Vale of Leven, called the Attacoti. Now by all accounts these folk were famous cannibals. With the wild, wet weather, the rugged terrain, the lack of food supplies and the Attacoti licking their lips deep in the ancient Caledonian forest it has to be said that north was not an inviting direction.

Zelda Elliot
Paisley Road West, Glasgow

Zelda Elliot makes an interesting point about the barbarism, even cannibalism, of the Caledonian tribes being a factor in the decision to consolidate the north-western fringe of the Empire on the Forth–Clyde axis. However, I fear that simply won't do. In their campaigns in Germany the Romans joined in battle with ferocious, headhunting, possibly flesh-eating tribes and this never deflected them from their goal of routing barbarism wherever they found it. Even more significantly we should remember that within 100 miles of the Eternal City Roman armies had encountered cannibal tribespeople so the experience of being confronted by human flesh eaters is unlikely to have seriously affected any tactical decisions.

Julius Agricola McClung
Ninth Legion Re-enactment Group,
Roman Road, Bearsden

If you read Tacitus, son-in-law and spin doctor of the Roman general Agricola, and his reports of the Caledonian campaign in the first century AD, so much seems to focus around the famous Roman victory at Mons Graupius, in AD 84 or 85. And yet, what do we know of this battle? According to Tacitus, 10,000 Picts were slain and only 360 Romans – a stunning victory by any standards. But where did it take place? Many locations have claimed the battle site. The slopes of Bennachie in Aberdeenshire might have the best claim – a Roman camp was found nearby. But, as to remnants of the battle, as far as I know nothing significant has been uncovered at any of the suggested sites. Strange for such a mighty clash of arms, don't you think?

It is worth speculating that the Battle of Mons Graupius may have been merely a reported victory, an imaginary battle, portrayed as a crushing, epoch-making triumph which drew a line under the Roman expedition to the wild north of Britain. It was pictured as a final victory for the Empire.

You might wonder why, after such a decisive victory, Agricola did not press home his advantage and establish a permanent presence in the far north, putting all of Britain from the Pentland Firth to the English Channel under the sway of Rome. But I ask again – did the battle actually happen?

Pete Medden
14 Chariot Road, Back o' Bennachie, Aberdeenshire

Smiley Face

Whenever I meet Scots here in Greece, either on holiday or when they are following their football teams, they are forever optimistic, filled with cheerful confidence. Is this a national trait?

Ramadan Quit
Miro's Irish Bar, Knossos, Crete

I suspect the people that Mr Quit encountered might be filled with something stronger than cheerful confidence. The Scot in his natural state, either at home or abroad on holiday, is morose, introverted and clannish and it usually takes several refreshing glasses of something alcoholic to bring him out of his shell suit.

The Scot at play overseas has always been, to me, a terrifying sight. Ramadan Quit has been remarkably lucky not to see the other side of the coin. With single-minded determination, the aim seems to be to defeat everyone at beach football, in karaoke competitions, at sinking vast quantities of beer, making fun of other nations and behaving disgracefully. These Scots can never be described as optimistic, in my view, but blindly fatalistic, out to prove, apparently before it's too late, that we are the greatest small nation on earth and that we know how to party.

Our politicians will tell you that we are moving into a new age of confidence and well-being (I think there is even an institute in Glasgow dedicated to this unlikely concept) but try going to the folk in the dilapidated housing schemes in our cities with the optimistic message that they've never had it so good. They would laugh in your face.

There is a distinct feeling when you encounter the seemingly optimistic Scots that they know something we don't about the future of mankind. They party like there is no tomorrow, not in a laid-back, controlled manner, but in what seems to be a mad rush to oblivion. If they do know something, I wish they would let the rest of us in on it.

Jack Duff
c/o Temperance Hotel, Linlithgow

Following many years' research at our institute into the attitudes of people within countries from Nepal to the

Falkland Isles, and having had the pleasure of interviewing hundreds of Scots and Scots' descendants at Highland Games in the United States and Canada, I can say, without fear of contradiction, that I have found you Scots invariably filled with bright hopes, dreams and ambitions. I imagine my critics will say that the type of individual I have interviewed – clan chiefs, St Andrews club chairmen, politicians, journalists – have more reason than most to be positive and optimistic and are not representative of the overwhelming majority of urban Scots, but these fine folk tell me they are, and who am I to argue? My conclusion is that the Scots are indeed an optimistic people. Although when you look at their history you do wonder from whence that optimism flows.

Joy Bliss
The Institute for the Study of How to be Really Cheerful,
Happy Valley, Idaho

Having read Mr Duff's tragic letter I realise to my utter dismay that the creature from the black depths of the Scottish soul – the whine/cringe – is alive. Is Mr Duff living in the same country as the rest of us where, on a daily basis, we can now sense a fresh wind of national optimism running across Scotland?

As a former leader of the SNP once declared, Scotland is a blessed land with an environment unmatched anywhere in the world, historic world-class universities, high-tech industries and one of the most patient and versatile work forces on the planet. Our professionals – engineers, doctors, administrators, preachers and teachers – have helped shape the modern world. However, to mention these things in some quarters is clearly still seen as being 'bigsy', uncool and somehow un-Scottish. The sooner we shed this nonsense the better.

It is my firm belief that optimism and self-confidence builds on itself and I honestly believe that ball is rolling. Our Scottishness is no longer judged by how anti-English we are: it is assessed by our enterprise and knowledge of our great nation, its history, geography, culture and its people. We remain perhaps the most potent and influential – and optimistic – small nation in the world.

Ratchet McGowrie
MV *Pride of Prestonpans*, Red Sea

Tae See Wirsels . . .

Why, in the twenty-first century, does Scotland continue to hang on to its outmoded heather and haggis image? Is it fair to blame VisitScotland and Sir Walter Scott or do we all shoulder some of the responsibility?

Peter Ploy
Glebe Street, Broonstoon

Heather is beautiful, haggis is tasty (so is shortbread for that matter), whisky is grand and tartan is trendy. Our tourist trade brings in umpteen millions of pounds annually. Why the need for this persistent navel-gazing over our image? So the power brokers are worried that we give the impression internationally of a nation stuck in the past. So what? Certainly most of those icons are of Highland origin but I, for one, feel no guilt about this and, as far as I'm concerned, we have nothing to be ashamed of. The world seems to love us as we are. Is that not enough? After all, we could be like the English – who are universally disliked, who totally lack any sense of national identity beyond the football field and who are united only by a love of Noel Edmonds and Mr Blobby.

Malcolm McDuff
Caledonia Rise, Innertoon, Edinburgh

You have to say that Scotland is a crock of conflicting images. We try to tell folk we are a cool, modern nation, locked into the technology and ideas of the twenty-first century but then we confuse the world and ourselves by publicly identifying our Scottishness with tartan and heather kitsch – and all, it seems, for the Yankee dollar.

VisitScotland, in particular, I think, must find themself in a bind over this. The people who come here from the world over want confirmation of the received image of Scotland that has travelled the globe over the past century and a half. They want Mel Gibson riding through the glen, hair flowing in the breeze, or Rob Roy putting one over on the damned English (Scottish Lowlanders in fact). It is the world of Bruce and Wallace, of Mary, Queen of Scots and Bonnie Prince Charlie, of Sir Walter Scott, Robbie Burns and Harry Lauder, of sea-girt castles, swishing kilts and couthy country folk. That is the Scotland they want.

There is an old saying that the customer is always right. If so, we must take a deep breath and give them precisely that. After all, it's horses for courses, really. The agencies trying to attract high-tech industry to this country tend to wisely sidestep the couthy heilan' hame image of Scotland and concentrate on the adaptability and skills of the Scottish workforce. But, on the other hand, it would be a foolish Scotch whisky company indeed that ignored the power of Highland imagery in promoting its product.

I fear as long as tartanry and its camp followers are such money-spinners then our shiny new Scotland will have to share the stage with Harry Lauder's cromach.

Fyfe N. Drum
Managing Director, Tartan-A-Go-Go, High Street, Banff

The tartan smokescreen which hides the real Scotland is a product of a number of events which took place in the eighteenth and nineteenth centuries. To understand the tartan creed of today we must look back.

The cult of Highlandism, what Professor Tom Devine has called 'quite literally the invention of a tradition', began within a few years of the final defeat of the clans at Culloden. The English middle classes were thirsting for nostalgia and, frankly, weren't too fussy about its authenticity. The Scottish Gael had been tamed and his wild home ground was now a safe and suitable playground – exotic yet close, different and interesting. The exploits of Scots soldiers in the British army, the Ossian sagas 'unearthed' by James Macpherson, both contributed. The Highlander and his tartan were rehabilitated and a myth was born. With Victoria and Albert on Royal Deeside, the royal seal of approval was applied.

That this was a remarkable, substantial and potent creation is evidenced by its continuing presence in contemporary Scottish society. However, there must be strenuous efforts made to ensure that the world knows a genuine, forward-looking Scotland seeking its place in the new century does exist.

If some wish to attach blame for the continuation of the myth and seek its destruction then they must always be reminded that this myth today helps keep thousands of people in employment at the heart of one of the nation's most important industries – tourism.

Duane Lockerbie
Department of National Stereotypes,
University of the Bronx, New York, New York

Good Neighbours?

By calling our English neighbours 'Sassenachs', am I using a term of abuse or affection? Likewise am I being offensive by calling Highlanders 'teuchters'?

Susie Concord
Harmony Row, Govan, Glasgow

Sassenach is a complex word but, if you check the dictionaries, Susie, you'll find its origin is in the Gaelic *Sasunnach*, which refers specifically to English speakers. It will come as no surprise to learn that the word was applied by Highlanders to everyone who spoke English, including the Lowland Scots. So I fear, Susie, you too are a Sassenach. For the dwellers in the glens the Lowlanders might as well have been English, having adopted the language, culture and superior airs and graces of the sooth. It is not a complimentary nickname.

Hamish the Highlander
2 Bon Accord Way, Kelso

For what it's worth I think there has been an unfortunate mix-up somewhere along the line here. I've a feeling the word the Scots started using of the English all those centuries ago was not *sasunnach* but something very similar – *sassenger*. Alas, this doesn't clarify the situation much because this old Scots word means sausage. And why on earth would we be calling our dear cousins south of the Border sausages?

William A. Cumberland
The Links, Andouillette, France

Lowland Scots, who long ago took the English silver, have always been in the habit of bad-mouthing Highlanders. It's in their nature. The precise meaning of teuchter is a matter of much debate but take it from me that every time I've heard it used it in the last fifty years in relation to Gaelic speakers or Highlanders it has not been as a compliment! Books of music for the Great Highland bagpipe are often titled tutors and one story is that Lowland soldiers of a Highland regiment passing the band hut heard the pipe major making reference to tutors or teuchters and the nickname stuck. On the other hand, the *Concise Scots Dictionary* has teuch as an adjective meaning tough or coarse. Take yer pick!

Rorie Hunterston
Fortress Grampian, Kingussie, Inverness-shire

There is no doubt that, over the years, the word Sassenach has come to mean something different than simply an English speaker. It seems to have been corrupted by common usage. For most Scots it quite specifically means 'the English'. I would say it is a term of contempt — Ed.

Thieving Scots

You Scots have laid doubtful claim to King Arthur, placing Camelot in Central Scotland. It is now being suggested that Robin Hood was a Scot. Is there any other part of the English heritage you'd like to pilfer?

Rev. Roger Pedant
Bury St Edmunds, Suffolk

Doubtful? I'll give you doubtful. Many respected scholars are now of the opinion that the biggest myth about Arthur and the Knights of the Round Table is that their stomping ground was somewhere in the South of England.

Brittany, Cornwall, Wales and Cumberland all lay claim to him but increasingly the evidence suggests that Arthur was a Strathclyde Briton, with his capital at the rock fortress of Dumbarton. Legends of Arthurian connections abound throughout Central Scotland. Rather than a king in the modern sense, Arthur would have been a tribal leader. He was a P-Celt or, put more simply, a Briton, and a military commander, fighting the Q-Celt Scots recently arrived from Ireland, the Saxons and the Picts to the north-east. Strathclyde, we know, stretched from present-day Lancashire to the north end of Loch Lomond where, in Glen Falloch, you can visit the Stone of the Britons.

It would certainly be wrong to describe Arthur as a Scot – the nation as we know it today did not exist in the sixth century. But as to having stolen him . . . you cannot steal what is yours in the first place.

By the same token we didn't have to pinch Robin Hood. Even in England it is generally accepted that Robin of Locksley, Robin Hood, was the creation of the medieval English spin doctors, trying to restore national confidence after the devastation of the Black Death. It should be obvious to anyone who has read the epic adventures of William Wallace where they got their inspiration.

Little John Flynn
Chief Frier, The Hungry Haddock,
Port of Menteith, Stirlingshire

You'll hear it said that there is no hard evidence that Robin Hood actually existed but it's strange that the first three mentions of the bold Nottingham boy come in the work of Scottish medieval chroniclers. It's just possible that he existed in some literary form south of the Border but the likelihood is that Scots writers brought him to life and created the legend and he was re-exported as a folk hero. As John Flynn has so accurately stated, anyone examining the story can't help but notice similarities with the life of William Wallace. Further evidence of this theory may be seen in the popularity of 'Robin Hood' plays in medieval Scotland.

Dr Turbot Charge
Museum of Folk Heroes, Penny Lane, Port Glasgow

This debate over the identity and origins of Robin Hood is fascinating. Suddenly all is becoming clear. Robin of Locksley was indeed a Scot. And when you think of it, could any Englishman have been so brave and self-sacrificing? Ah hae me doots! If we needed further confirmation the words of the song tell it all:

> Robin Hood, Robin Hood, riding through the glen,
> Robin Hood, Robin Hood, with his band of men,
> Feared by the bad, loved by the good,
> Robin Hood, Robin Hood, Robin Hood.

Walter Sheriff
The Green Wood, Helmsdale, Ross and Cromarty

4
Sea and sky

With Their Boots On

*For years now I have wanted to work on the trawlers operating out of
one of the north-east of Scotland's ports. I leave school this summer
but I'm unable to swim and have been told that unless I learn I will
have no chance of landing a job. Is this true?*

Sylvia Hake
The Trout Ladder, Water of Leith, Edinburgh

How very brave of you, for all sorts of reasons, Sylvia, to
be considering a career in fishing at what is a desperately
difficult time for the industry – particularly in Scotland with
quota restrictions and decommissioning. The fact that you
are female, if I may be politically incorrect for a moment,
makes your decision all the more remarkable. For all the
much-improved conditions on board trawlers these days,
it is still difficult and dangerous work in an unforgiving
environment.

As to the business of whether you should be able to swim
or not, I think you'll find that most government organisations
and fishing representatives would now strongly urge that you
learn to swim.

As you hinted, that was not always the case. It is true that
in centuries past many fishermen in Scotland, indeed many
people dwelling along the coast, never saw much point in

learning to swim. The logic was that if you went overboard in heavy sea boots and working gear you would sink to the bottom – struggling to swim would only prolong the agony. Rescue in times past was unlikely. Nowadays, with survival gear and high-tech search and rescue helicopters capable of being on the scene rapidly, it is a different story. New safety measures and devices are regularly being introduced. One of the most recent is a floating steel cage which the man (or woman) overboard can swim to for sanctuary while awaiting rescue.

The sea is a dangerous mistress but we are slowly putting her in her place.

Capt. Bob Grilse (retired)
The Cutlass Bar and Grill, Penzance, Cornwall

I was interested in Captain Grilse's response to the young lady who wanted to take up a career in deep-sea fishing. His explanation as to why so many fishermen in centuries past never learned to swim tells only half the story.

Scottish fishermen may indeed have been fatalistic about their chances of survival but we should never forget that they had a cold and dangerous sea at their doorstep in which to learn to swim, unlike their counterparts in the warmer Mediterranean lands who would be in the water from a very young age. Learning to swim in the grey North Sea was a brave option.

But there is something much deeper than this at work in this reluctance to learn to swim. Primitive people must surely have felt totally powerless against the awesome, primeval fury of the northern seas. It was a hostile force beyond human control. Swimming was indeed pointless. These days, ships are so impressive, crammed with the most up-to-date technical equipment imaginable to keep the ocean in its place. Like Captain Bob above writes, it does occasionally seem that we are no longer awed by the sea. Then along comes the Christmas tsunami which devastates a large area of the globe and explodes our complacency. The sea remains awesome, beyond our control.

Lucky Harding
14 The Waterfront, Anstruther, Fife

Learning to swim may seem a small act in the face of such wrath but learn anyway, Sylvia, even if it's just to please your parents — Ed.

On the Rocks

With global warming, how soon can we expect to see icebergs off Cape Wrath?

Smiler McDaid
The Snug, *The Ploughman's Thighs*, Ochiltree, Ayrshire

Depending which expert you listen to, the average temperatures in Scotland over the next seventy-five years will rise by between 3°C and 6°C. This will be accompanied by a significant rise in sea level as a result of the melting of the ice caps, a phenomenon which already seems to be well under way. Signs that this process is already happening are all around you in Scotland. To take just one startling, yet simple, example, the song of the thrush, which is the traditional herald of spring, is now being heard at Christmas.

Currently the American, and to a lesser extent the British, government is running away from the idea that there is a problem. They argue in the face of all the evidence about mankind's production of greenhouse gases and its contribution to warming that there may be a totally natural explanation for these changes.

What we will never see are flotillas of icebergs floating serenely south past Cape Wrath or out from the Beach Boulevard in Aberdeen. Warming will mean that these bergs break up and disintegrate long before reaching our coast as they pass through the tepid waters of the North Atlantic.

But other effects will be equally dramatic and may change the whole face of Scotland long before the century's end. With the sort of temperature changes that are being predicted it seems possible that Royal Deeside may rival Burgundy, with a string of vineyards producing some of the finest wines in Europe (Château Balmoral and Côtes du Braemar); already bananas are being domestically cultivated in Fife; spring and autumn will disappear and the mountaintops of Scotland may never see snow.

Increased temperatures could mean that mosquitoes, butterflies and poisonous spiders will begin to make the long trek north. On the plus side, the growing season will have increased impressively and a wider range of crops should be possible. As birdlife adjusts to changes, new species will appear and long-established species will vanish.

As the sea level rises, low-lying areas, for example in Orkney, will start to disappear beneath the waves and the whole geography of the Scottish coastline will change. The policy of placing nuclear power plants along the Scottish shoreline, as at Hunterston, Chapelcross and Dounreay, will now appear to have been short-sighted and possibly catastrophic.

There is every chance that a global refugee crisis will develop as a billion people flee low-lying places from East Anglia to South East Asia – and Scotland will have to be ready to take her share. We may find ourselves playing host to the entire population of Holland. Although the Scottish uplands will be an attractive target for climate change refugees there are also likely to be fearsome heat waves even here which will cost thousands of lives, similar to the unexpected disaster which overtook France in the scorching summer of 2003.

All in all this is not an inspiring prospect (the Scottish Beaujolais aside). Just be glad that the vast majority of you will no longer be around to see the new, balmy Scotland of the twenty-second century.

Ulpian Mott
Global Warming Watch,
6 Mittelstrasse, Hamburg, Germany

Personally, I believe there is far too much scaremongering in relation to global warming. Over the piece my belief is that Scotland stands to gain substantially from the great changes already under way – even though we are unlikely to witness icebergs floating by. With the Mediterranean countries baking under a sun which will turn places like the Côte d'Azur into arid, semi-desert regions, Scotland will come into its own as the trendy new European holiday destination. St Andrews will be the new St Tropez, North Berwick the Antibes of East Lothian. Many crucial issues will have to be decided. Should the Scottish Executive introduce legislation to make the siesta compulsory and will we allow German tourists to leave their towels on beach recliners in order to stake an early slot in the sun?

Professor Peter Pepper
School of Catastrophe Studies,
The Bunker, Halfway Up Ben Lomond, Stirlingshire

Call of the Wild

Why do there seem to be fewer mysterious 'big cats' on the loose in Scotland in comparison with the southern counties of England? And where are all of Scotland's phantom dogs?

Terence Wolfe
13 Rozilla Road, Torquay, Devon

Mr Wolfe is correct in noting the absence of phantom dogs in Scotland. I have a theory about this canine conundrum.

While south of the Border you do indeed seem to be tripping over legendary Black Dogs, there is a genuine dearth of spectral hounds here in Scotland, a land which is, let's face it, generally thought to have more supernatural phenomena than is good for us. We have grey or green ladies, headless horsemen, phantom backpackers, haunted houses by the street-full, not to mention wraiths, kelpies, bogles, brownies, forest spirits and trolls, but, yes, surprisingly few demoniacal dugs.

In England almost every county has a Black Dog legend which has become so much a part of people's experience that some of the beasties have their own names – the Black Shuck in Norfolk or the Gurt Dog in Somerset. Wherever these stories surface they have a remarkable similarity. People speak of a fearful creature stalking old tracks, churchyards and crossroads; the sight of these mutts was apparently enough to make you faint with horror.

Returning to my theory – I reckon that these creatures were missing from Scottish folklore because, up until a couple of hundred years ago, we had our very own flesh-and-blood devil dogs. What need for flights of fancy when we had our own hungry, slavering, child-devouring Caledonian wolf?

Rolf Ravnus
Granny's Pantry, Glencoe, Argyll

Whit's a' this aboot a dearth o' spooky dugs? The legends almost certainly did have their origins, as Mr Ravnus suggests, in a time when wolves caused havoc up and doon the glens. But wi' a wee bit o' basic research it's easy enough to come up with some crackin' examples of the Black Dog north o' the Border. There's a ghost dog in Breadalbane which accompanied travellers along the shore of Loch Tay; at Cromarty there is a tale of a phantom pack of hounds; Arran has the Red Hound of Altanourn Woods and Lochwinnoch in Renfrewshire has its own SPD (Suspected Black Dog).

My own favourite though is the Crusader Hound of Barnbougle Castle, just west of Edinburgh on the shore near Dalmeny. The story is that the castle got its name from the dreadful wail of a dog whose spectre has patrolled the vicinity since the days of the Crusades. The dog went with its master to the Holy Land and its pitiful wail was heard at the precise moment his master was struck down – and has been heard on and off ever since.

Grant Tucker
The Dog House, Bonnybridge Road, Coupar Angus

Big cats are a well-established feature of the British landscape and have been now for thirty years. Sightings have been numerous and detailed. Specimens have been captured, notably one at Inverness, and they are clearly at large and breeding in our countryside, posing, according to some experts, an ever-increasing threat to domestic animals and human beings.

The big cats are thought to be descended from pets released into the wild after the introduction of the Dangerous Wild Animals Act in 1976, which made it illegal to keep such creatures. It is known that well-off owners in the south released their animals into the English countryside and in a much more densely populated area they were always much more likely to be observed going about their business.

My own feeling is that there are big cats out there in the Scottish mountains which are generally well away from human gaze in the vast mountain fastnesses but which do stray into more populated areas from time to time. Perhaps the most famous was the so-called Beast of Bennachie. It was seen over a wide area around Inverurie in Aberdeenshire, which gave rise to the idea that there was more than one big cat in the vicinity, though experts confirmed that this creature might patrol a vast territory. Animals resembling the puma, lynx, mountain lion or cougar have all been sighted across Scotland.

It seems possible to me that these cats, which were released in the late 1970s, may have mated with Highland wildcats to produce a new strain of cat, which has yet to be properly identified but gives rise to stories of big, black cats.

Ros Leadbetter
Cats R Us, Main Street, Crieff

By Yon Bonnie Banks

Why does there seem to be so much doubt about how many islands there are in Loch Lomond? Since it is now the focus of a National Park is it not high time someone went out there and counted them?

Peter Brown
The Pepper Mill, South Park Road, Giffnock

Whenever we hear Loch Lomond mentioned it is usually because it is the largest expanse of fresh water in the United Kingdom, at some 27 square miles. At 23 miles it is also Scotland's third longest loch, after Loch Awe and Loch Ness, and varies between five miles and half a mile in width. Gouged out by glaciers in the Ice Age, it is shallow at its southern end where most of the islands are located but up to 700 feet deep in its narrow northern defile.

The question of the number of islands in the loch is something which has been a source of controversy over the years but a general consensus of reports and studies suggest that there may be as few as twenty-four islands or as many as forty. These vary from rocky outcrops to substantial, populated islands such as Inchmurrin, one and a half miles long by one mile wide.

A three-part proverb of Loch Lomond says it has waves without wind (swells which persist even after winds have subsided), fish without fins (probably grass snakes or eels) and a floating isle.

The most tantalising mystery of Loch Lomond's islands relates to this legend of a floating isle or isles, rather than a vanishing island as some might suggest. I think we will find that this enigma is tied up with the fact that there are a number of what we might call pseudo-islands in the loch. These include rocky outcrops which appear or disappear depending on the seasonal depth of the loch.

But, more importantly for the floating island legend, large rafts of vegetation are also reported from time to time and these may have been mistaken for permanent islets. Another possibility is that the mystery isles are a race memory of Neolithic floating crannogs, or loch houses, built on wooden rafts.

The answer will probably always remain a mystery.

Brian Mitchell
Bruce's Cave, Inversnaid, Loch Lomondside

After drinking rather too much than was good for us in Balloch, my mates and myself went out in a speedboat on Loch Lomond one magnificent July evening a few years back. Our intention was to see if the nudist colony on Inchmurrin was still up and running. Maybe a mile south of the island we passed a bulky object which seemed to swiftly rise from the water before equally quickly sinking back beneath the surface. The only way I can describe it is to say that it was like the back of a huge whale rising from the deep. We all saw it but never mentioned this to anyone in case they thought we were bonkers. I have to admit, that same night the boys thought they saw wee kangaroos running about on one of the smaller islands, so the drink may have been to blame right enough.

Horatio Gaffney
Drumry Road, Clydebank

I don't know about the mysterious creature rising from the deep (there are no legends of a Loch Lomond monster) but a wild colony of wallabies established itself on one of the islands in the 1970s after being set free, so Mr Gaffney and his mates might well have caught sight of the descendants of these creatures — Ed.

The High Life

Was high-rise housing, multi-storey residential buildings, in which I'm told Scotland led the way for Europe, really such a bad idea?

Ernest Slater
15th Floor, Paradise Court, Ecclefechan

It is fashionable now to descry the hundreds of multi-storey blocks of flats which shot up all over Scotland in the 1960s. The images of these flats now being demolished in spectacular, stage-managed explosions helps confirm the perception that they were a blot on both Scotland's physical and social landscapes.

In the immediate post-war period it became clear that drastic action would be needed to deal with the huge, decaying slum areas which blighted Glasgow. By the end of the 1950s around 100,000 families were on Glasgow's housing waiting list. Drastic action was called for and drastic action was certainly taken. As Professor Tom Devine has pointed out, a survey by Glasgow's town clerk had revealed 700,000 people living in 1,800 acres around the city centre, which meant that an incredible one third of the entire population of West Central Scotland was crammed into a three-square-mile bottleneck in the centre of the city.

The answer, in Glasgow and other Scottish cities, was to build peripheral housing schemes and these, of course, included many tower blocks. Somehow the word 'skyscraper' never really caught on here as a way of describing these high-rise developments. The post-war housing crisis meant that houses had to be built quickly – and cheaply. And they were. Multi-storey flats represented not just a better, cleaner, healthier life for the former tenement dwellers but they were a symbol of a final break with the squalor of the inner city slums.

The planners, in their anxiety to make improvements, certainly didn't take into account the social dislocation these new buildings would bring about. Gone were most of the closes where communities had grown. It was much more difficult in these soulless towers to get to know your neighbours – even on the same landing. However, I would say that the planners, by and large, were genuinely filled with the best of intentions.

I was brought up in a tower block and while I loved to look out from our front room across the south side of the city to the hills behind Clydebank there were others in these blocks who were from day one virtually prisoners in their own homes. It's safe to say that Scotland did show Europe the way with high-rise housing and as with most pioneering endeavours, pain and strain was part of the package.

Vincent Conroy
Institute for the Study of Very Tall Buildings,
High Blantyre, Lanarkshire

They're knocking the high flats down left, right and centre these days. They were a terrible mistake, I hear some experts cry. Yes, it's true that not nearly enough thought went into how communities, dragged from their inner city setting, could be rebuilt in the new schemes. It's my guess they thought such communities would grow organically. That theory proved to be incorrect.

What might be overlooked in the condemnation is that most people moving to these smart, new flats were leaving squalor, dereliction and overcrowding behind for a new life filled with expectation. Sadly, in too many cases, these dreams were not fulfilled but the building programme represented the great hope of the inner city dwellers. By all means criticise the thoughtless rush to reconstruct but let's recognise that something had to be done.

Ricky McNeil
Palace Road, Arbroath, Angus

Here, wait a minute – Glasgow first with the multi-storey flat? I think not. It is known that in sixteenth- and seventeenth-century Edinburgh, crowded as the Old Town was on the Castle ridge, the citizens reached for the skies to attempt to cure the problem of overcrowding in the heart of the nation's capital. Some of the rickety old buildings running down the spine of the ridge, down the High Street and its many closes, were said to have been fourteen storeys high.

Pat Faskally
Eight Miles High, The Promenade, Portobello

It was surely one of the great tragedies of the twentieth century that so many basically sound and salvageable tenement buildings in Glasgow went under the demolisher's hammer in the 1960s along with the notorious slum properties. But it has to be accepted that the rush to rehouse the slum dwellers was done for very positive social reasons. Now, after half a century, housing projects in Glasgow are being driven by local people who at last are having a full say in the shape of their community. The idea of multi-storey blocks has gone forever, lamented only by the few demented souls who thought that high living brought them closer to God — Ed.

The Morning Dew

Scots seem to be taking May Day as a festival much more seriously in recent years. Is there any obvious reason for this?

Dagda McDougall
The Sanctuary, Asda Car Park, Inverness

There is absolutely no doubt that the old Celtic festival of Beltane is beginning to catch the imagination of those for whom orthodox religion has lost its appeal. The truth is that we pagans know how to party. If you had been up and about at first light in our capital city of Edinburgh on May Day you would know that. Maidens washing their faces in the morning dew was the least of the excitement.

Edna McStume
High Priestess, Druidic Order of the Rampant Goat,
Garthamlock, Glasgow

If you ever thought that these Beltane events were a passing phase then you must think again. Local authorities are now supporting the Beltane festival which constitutes one of the most important ancient Celtic festivals, pre-dating Christianity and heralding the start of summer, effectively the end of winter and the commencement of the growing season. Giant bonfires were lit to protect cattle and crops against disease and to ward off witches and bad fairies who got mobile in the spring. These gatherings are based on age-old fertility rites and the cleansing and blessing of the May Queen before her May Day coronation. The festival is said to have included a sacrificial bonfire.

In my tender youth I was always confused by the co-relation between May Day as an important date in the ancient Celtic calendar and the world day of worker solidarity that it also seems to signify. The connection was just too subtle to unravel – that is until I discovered there was no connection at all. The simple fact is that May is the anniversary of the Russian Revolution in 1917.

Leaders of the Christian community in Scotland do not seem too downhearted by this sudden interest in the May Day celebration, which brings folk out in their thousands at a time when next to no one can be persuaded to become a regular churchgoer. But, if I were them, I would be worried.

The pagan Beltane festival is exciting, sexy, noisy, colourful, entertaining. The Church will struggle to match these attractions.

It is as well for practising Christians to accept that religion in Scotland didn't start with the arrival of the first Christian missionaries. It would also be very foolish of the Kirk to be in any way complacent about these developments. An older religion was already in place, rooted in society with its own traditions and superstitions, its own cycle of festivals and ceremonies. That these are slowly resurfacing is surely no great surprise in this rapidly changing world. To the pagan there was no certainty that the Lord or Lords would provide: he had to be appeased.

Carol San Diego
Party Till You Drop, Haight Ashbury, Kinfauns Drive, Drumchapel, Glasgow

These days the essential ingredients of the Beltane celebrations seem to be fire swinging, juggling, ferocious drumming (loud enough certainly to awaken the old Celtic gods – are you listening, Lug my boy?) and as much alcohol as the body can stand. I wonder if they were so different 2,000 years ago. The huge Edinburgh Beltane event of recent years reminds me very much of watching Mungo Jerry at the West of Scotland Rugby Club marquee dance in nineteen umpteen – a truly surreal experience, almost spiritual in its intensity. Nowadays the really hardy pagans dance the night away and are still around on Calton Hill to see the sun rise on May Day morning. Oddly, one of the most unlikely settings for Beltane celebrations is in the English university city of Oxford. A typical Beltane bash might see a Scottish student detained for indecent exposure and eighy-three students, many in dinner jackets and evening gowns after Beltane balls, leaping twenty feet into the River Cherwell. Fines of up to £500 can be levied for this ambitious leap — Ed.

⊙ Home Sweet Home Tae Me

What are the Northern Lights and when precisely are they switched on?

Lucas Gill
Tunbridge Wells, Devon

The story used to be told in Aberdeen about the visitor who asked when the Northern Lights are switched on. I always considered this to be an urban myth but now Mr Gill pops up to prove that we must never jump to conclusions. Can I be the first in what I'm sure will be a lengthy discourse attempting to enlighten your correspondent about the Northern Lights or, as they are known scientifically, the aurora borealis.

The technical account of the Lights describes them as resulting from the emanation of particles from the sun moving towards the earth at high velocity and being ionised during the passage. Under the influence of the earth's magnetic field a great number of the particles move towards the South and North Poles. The spectacular luminosity is caused when the particles collide with the gases of the upper atmosphere.

So there – noo ye ken! As to describing these lights for people who have never seen them, that is a task which I consider way beyond my literary skills and which I will leave to others better qualified than myself.

Anton Birse
The Observatory, St Kilda

Ignorance about the Northern Lights south of the Border is something which annoys the Scots but which, to my mind, is perfectly understandable. Seeing such an event that far south is such a rare happening and certainly in the crowded urban areas of England there is so much light pollution that even if the aurora put in an appearance the whole effect would be lost.

It is natural then that people should be sceptical, or indeed ignorant, about something which, by the descriptions, must seem almost supernatural, or, as Mr Gill seems to believe, part of some summer illuminations along Aberdeen's Beach Boulevard.

Richey Fyfe
Yardley Villas, Airbles Road, Motherwell

Best I can do in describing the aurora borealis is to quote from some of the descriptions left in our visitor's book here at the Poetry Corner:

> 'sweeping bands of yellow and green tinged light rushing across the winter sky . . .'
> 'a bluish arc formed across the starlit sky from which came great shafts of whiter light.'
> 'a colourful cascade of light radiating from a splendid crown.'
> 'a delicate rosy glow washed across the starry ceiling.'
> 'coronas were formed and glowing stairways seemed to descend from the heavens'
> 'we saw luminous bands of light swinging rapidly across the night sky giving the illusion they emanate from some distant searchlight.'

From the above it will be clear that viewing the aurora borealis is very close to a spiritual experience. I have known it to change the perspective of some of the most cynical and down-to-earth people you might meet.

Evan McCromish
Muckle Flugga Poetry Corner, Shetland

I particularly like the ancient legend that the lights were reflections of sunlight glinting off the chariots of the Valkyrie as they rushed across the night sky taking slain Norse warriors to Valhalla. For several centuries it has been claimed that the Northern Lights make a crackling sound during an aurora display. The number of witnesses who were eating smoky bacon crisps at the time casts some doubt on the authenticity of this associated phenomenon — Ed.

A Rock and a Hard Place

What do your readers consider to be the loneliest location in Scotland? For me the summit of the Cairngorms have the feel of another world right on our doorstep.
Napthalon Bomb
Abbey of St Alex the French Polisher, Beauvais, France

Speaking from bitter experience, unquestionably the loneliest place not just in Scotland but on the planet can be the last coach of a late-night train out of Glasgow. If you happen to be corralled with a drunk it can be an experience never to be forgotten. Even a bus seems somehow less menacing. When those coach doors on the train slide shut you're riding your luck as well as a train.

If St Christopher is smiling, you might have a sleepy drunk who sprawls opposite you, chin on chest, singing football anthems or Shania Twain hits to himself as the train rattles through the night. If you're a little less lucky then your travelling companion, between the aforementioned songs, will aggressively regale you with stories of his previous career as a taxi driver, debt collector or clergyman. If you're out of luck then the person with the hollow eyes opposite will ask you all sorts of questions you really know you shouldn't be answering. Which stop are you getting off, would you like a swig o' ma vodka, have you got a boyfriend/girlfriend, weren't we at school together, do ye mind if I sit next to you? Having identified the nearest emergency cord you look out of the window at the houses and cars rushing by, wishing you were sitting in the passenger seat listening to the CD player or curled up in an armchair in front of the telly behind one of those thousands of windows. In fact, you are wishing you were anywhere but in that bloody train.

Yes, I'm sure lots of folk will nominate the top of Ben Lomond, or St Kilda and suchlike places but they are most often beautifully, mercifully empty. Oh, that my night-time railway coach was as deserted.

Sam Coupling
Platform 6, Bridgeton Central Station, Glasgow

Rockall is unquestionably the loneliest place in Scotland but is too small to make even a contour on the largest-scale maps and, until the middle of the twentieth century, its exact location was not certain. In fact the seventy-foot-high granite outcrop lies 289 miles west of the Scottish mainland.

The history of Rockall consists of confirmed fact, conjecture, half-truths and downright lies. The outcrop is all that is visible of a land formation that once marked the northern limit of the Atlantic at a period when it was separated from the great Arctic Basin. There are some claims and several tall stories. Enthusiasts had tried to swim ashore but were defeated until a military landing in the 1950s.

It is about 450 years since Rockall began to appear, inaccurately, on maps and charts. As part of a sea story it has its first mention from Martin Martin who, while rent collecting on St Kilda in 1697, heard of the crew of a French or Spanish vessel which had been wrecked on 'Rokol' and had come to Hirta in a pinnace. The waters around the rock were charted in 1745 and, in 1811, while HMS *Endymion* was lying near and 'we had nothing better on our hands', Basil Hall, a lieutenant, took a landing party to the islet and succeeded in scaling the rock. The adventure became troublesome when a mist came down and they were for many hours unable to rejoin the ship.

Fifty years later, as fishing was developing in the area, HMS *Porcupine* was detailed to make soundings in the Rockall Bank and, on a fair day, a boat was sent to the rock, bringing back the first geological specimens. The rock was on the map but has remained a remarkably remote and atmospheric place.

Sarah Swashy
Briny Path, Castlebay, Barra

I was interested to read Sarah Swashy's opinion that Rockall must be the loneliest spot in Scotland. Funnily enough it has only qualified for such a status within the last half-century. It was in 1955 to be exact that Rockall was claimed, annexed by a team of British commandos because of its strategic importance in the North Atlantic fishery. They landed on the summit from a cable hanging from a helicopter, claiming it in the name of the Queen, and confirmed the new status by cementing a plaque to the rock face. I can imagine the missionary/explorer St Brendan's first reaction on seeing Rockall: 'So this is Atlantis, not much to write home to the boys about.' So he didn't and headed off instead in the direction of Iceland.

Hector Scanlan
Fixtures Secretary, The South Devon Beach Volley Ball League, Teignmouth, Devon

Light on the Matter

What was, or is, the Lamp of Lothian? My wife says it is the lighthouse on the Bass Rock in the Forth. True or false?

Eddie Ray
Candlewick Green, Brighton, Sussex

It's possible that I'm going a bit senile or maybe I took one too many smacks tae the heid but I could swear that one of the best boxers to come out Dalkeith – Johnny 'Wide Boy' Lafferty – was nicknamed the Lamp o' Lothian because of the number of opponents he floored after lamping them with his haymaker of a left mitt. As I say my recollections are a bit hazy.

Bertie 'Burst Lip' Tulloch
The Drill Hall, Bridgeton Cross, Glasgow

The Bass Rock at the gateway to the River Forth could quite reasonably be titled the Light of Lothian, Mr Ray, but the Lamp of Lothian is without question the name given to the medieval Franciscan church beside the River Tyne at Haddington in East Lothian, and in particular to its impressive square tower. The name was retained with the construction of St Mary's Church of the Virgin, now St Mary's Collegiate Church. Along with St Giles in Edinburgh and St Michael's in Linlithgow, it is considered one of the three great medieval churches in the Lothians. Historians suggest that St Mary's may also have earned its nickname because of its central role in the Christian community of East Lothian.

Dr Miles Long
Director, Institute for Really Neat Church Buildings,
Bitter-Le-Will, Notts.

I am surprised and disappointed to find your publication once again giving a platform to Glasgow's lowlife (of which there are many). For 'Burst Lip' Tulloch to get our wonderful church of St Mary's at Haddington confused with some deadbeat pugilist from Dalkeith really shows the failings of the educational system in the West of Scotland. It also confirms a view held by many in our capital city that there must be something in the air or in the water on Clydeside. How else do we account for this basic denseness in the West of Scotland populace? It can't only be inbreeding. But, in the spirit of conciliation and goodwill, if Mr Ray and his fellow scrappers would like to contact me I will arrange to have them shown around the church at Haddington.

Felix Snark
MSP for the Posh Parts of Edinburgh,
The Upturned Boats, by Holyrood

5

Kings and commoners

In Love with Royalty

Why does Scotland seem to be so much in love with royalty and the London-based British royal family in particular?

Hugo 'Scratcher' Boyle
Vehicle 22, Dawsholm Incinerator Plant, Glasgow

I wonder if you are correct, Hugo, about the intensity of this love affair. If I sense the mood in Scotland correctly these days there is a distinct cooling towards the Windsors. This latest spat began with the Queen's Jubilee when, if memory serves me correctly, while England went into a frenzy of street parties and flag waving, Scotland was positively tepid about the whole business.

More recently you could put this lack of interest, apathy even, down to a fresh burst of democracy and people power since the advent of the new Parliament in Edinburgh or you might relate it to the questionable antics of the Royals themselves. Again, perhaps it may be that Scotland senses that before too long a new King or Queen of Scots will be required.

I would argue that over the centuries the Scottish people have been unquestionably the most supportive to the monarchy of the four nations of the United Kingdom. As historian Michael Fry has observed – Ireland only ever had tribal chieftains, Wales only ever had medieval princes and England has been the only nation to try a republic, under Oliver Cromwell (if not for long). Scotland alone has been continuously loyal to the royal line. As to why this should be, it is a bit of a mystery really, but if we look at the difference in the nature of kingship in Scotland and in England we might possibly find some sort of explanation. That this has been a special relationship is beyond question and it continued even after the Union of the Crowns in 1603, when James VI packed his bags and headed for London with, some might say, indecent haste. Yet his Scottish subjects did not bat an eyelid and after the Stuarts were deposed (by the English) later in the century the Scots spearheaded two botched attempts to restore them in the 1700s.

Even when the Scots seemed to have been forgotten by their king, they still kept the faith. No member of the royal family visited Scotland between 1681 and 1822, except the Duke of Cumberland in 1746 who was Culloden-bound.

Yes, we do seem to love our rulers – sometimes beyond all reason, but we do love them.

Countess Isla von Altschwanstein (née McGurk)
Schloss Gepacktrager, Salzburg, Austria

The Countess is surely correct in saying that Scotland's love of monarchy must relate to the way we have regarded kingship over the centuries. Since 1066 there has always been a King of England but there has never been a King of Scotland. Yes, you read correctly. The usage was always – King of Scots. To some this may appear to be an extreme example of splitting hairs but it is an absolutely fundamental distinction.

The Norman Conquest holds the key to this enigma. It was fully two centuries before the Norman arrivals felt they had satisfactorily pacified England. Control of the country depended on the ownership of the land by the king, held by right of conquest and divided up amongst his barons in return for loyalty and feudal service. Each of these noblemen had to provide, according to the extent of his land grant from the king, a specific number of knights, archers and foot soldiers. The king was quite literally King of England.

North of the Border, Scotland, without getting all misty-eyed and brave-hearted about it, was a land of free men. It had never been conquered. To the Scots the sovereign has always been looked on as 'a representative of the race' or a patriarch, very much in the style of the clan chiefs who were kinsmen to everyone in the clan. Little wonder then that we feel tied tightly to the monarchy.

Tim Martini-Royale
O'Rourke's Peerage, The Old Abattoir, Dalbeattie, Kirkcudbrightshire

⦿ Hail to the Chief

I think I have a claim to the throne of Scotland as a descendant of Bonnie Prince Charlie. In the right sort of light my brother Willie bears a striking resemblance to the Young Pretender. How do I go about proving I should be King?

Vincent 'Bugs' Longniddry
The Speckled Hen English Tea Shop, Rue de Rivoli, Paris, France

You should prepare first of all to join a very long queue of individuals who have convinced themselves that they are direct descendants of Bonnie Prince Charlie.

Why anyone in their right mind would want the hapless Stuarts restored to power is another matter.

However, you are following in very distinguished footsteps in seeking to place yourself on the throne of Scotland. As a matter of passing interest (a result of the Union of the Crowns), you would also have to become ruler of England, Wales and Ulster, which for some might make the job just that little bit less attractive.

The direct Stuart line is generally accepted to have ended with the death of Bonnie Prince Charlie and then his brother Henry, in 1807. Around this time the brothers John Stolberg Stuart and Charles Edward Stuart came to Edinburgh and were feted for many years as sons of the Young Pretender. Their family name was Sobieski and they were largely responsible for the invention of Scottish clan tartans, having published the *Vestarium* which they said was the transcript of a manuscript found at Douai in France containing tartans which no one had ever heard of or seen before. It transpired that the two pretenders were sons of a naval lieutenant and that they made the very best of a family resemblance to the Stuart royals.

There have been plenty of other folk claiming the title over the years since including Albrecht, Duke of Bavaria, the Duke of Buccleuch, various Highland estate owners including Mohammed Al Fayed and perhaps most interestingly a young Belgian aristocrat now based in Scotland who styles himself Prince Michael James Alexander Stuart of Albany. He holds an impressive CV which includes a claim that he is the great-great-great-great-grandson of Bonnie Prince Charlie and titular Prince of France and Holland.

Mary Bonny
Dunoon, Argyll

I wouldn't hold my breath on the restoration of the Stuarts or any other claimants. Most informed observers do agree that if Scotland does regain her independence the likelihood is that the monarchy will be retained in the new set-up – and it will be the House of Windsor. However, Vincent, if you are determined to give it a go, in my humble opinion it would be an immense help if, as well as the blood of Bonnie Prince Charlie, you had that of Billy Connolly, William Wallace, Mary Queen of Scots, Alex Salmond, John Maclean, Lulu, Sir Walter Scott, Jimmy Krankie, George IV and Tommy Sheridan coursing through your veins. Now there's a cocktail to conjure with. That would surely guarantee you the broad-based support of the people.

My initial advice in pressing your claim to the throne would be to get yourself a good genealogist – me, preferably – and probably a good lawyer also, but, most important of all, raise your standard at some God-forsaken loch, gather together a raggle-taggle army of about 6,500 wild Highlanders and, when you reach Derby . . . keep straight on for London this time. The Tartan Army have done all the reconnaissance work. England is there for the taking (whisper it – whether your credentials are bona fide or not!).

Pavel Surbiton
'Yer Ma's a Maori', Ancestor Finders, Maxwell Drive, Pollokshields, Glasgow

◉ Kill or Cure

My friend Oleg whose factory ship often visited Ullapool told me that Scottish hangover cures are worthless. He also says the English are more enthusiastic about whisky than the Scots. Can any of this be true?

Random Stem
Gutteral View, Lochinver, Sutherland

When the Russians tell us our cures are a waste of time then we should sit up and pay attention. They know a thing or two about drink survival, having had to suffer some seriously painful vodka concoctions over the years.

But this leads us to an aspect of Scottish drinking which might explain the lack of quality hangover cures – and that is the penitential hangover, one in which you quite deliberately avoid a cure.

What is this all about? It's a reminder in the fine Calvinist tradition which applies to the righteous and the down and out alike – i.e. punishment must follow pleasure just as surely as night follows day, or, as the Ettrick Shepherd James Hogg so neatly described it, 'how oft the evening cup of joy turns to sorrow in the morning'. It is my belief that a large number of Scots drinkers would abandon the drink habit if they were told that they could get away without the sorrow in the morning. As one observer has said, the Scots, a pragmatic people, have accepted the arrangement as a fair bargain. The hangover appeals to our sense of justice – play the game, take the knocks, don't complain. In fact we should cherish that familiar 'why don't you please just kill me and get it over with' feeling.

Filip Glass
The Reactor Bar, Dounreay, Caithness

Scots have always looked sceptically on so-called miracle hangover cures and with good reason. A few years ago, one of the pioneers in this field produced a sachet containing a certain kind of grit which, when placed in a bottle of wine or glass of spirits, immunised the drinker against ill effects. I had a friend who immediately latched on to this idea on the basis that he had never seen a drunken budgerigar.

As mentioned above, we Scots are a sceptical people and when the producers of this grit revealed it had come from the coral reefs of the Sea of Japan and was said also to improve the taste of any drink into which it was placed, gave long life, was good for gout and sleeplessness and helped you remember whose round it was, the Scots rejected it out of hand.

My own view is that there is nothing wrong with a hangover – it is to be suffered in silence. It's nature's way of telling you you've drunk too much.

As to emptying buckets of sand into your favourite drink – get ye tae Okinawa!

Sam 'The Cynic' Dunleavy
Block 'C', Peterhead Prison, Aberdeenshire

This suggestion that the Scots know little and care less about hangover cures is surely nonsense. The key to our drinking has always been prevention rather than cure. Scots chow barrowloads of bananas which provide a nutritious stomach lining prior to bevvying; we drink gallons of water which has a splendidly positive effect by controlling dehydration and, as a cure, we know the value of eating a hearty breakfast – preferably with porridge and white pudding; that is clearly the business. There are hundreds of other remedies but above all else you must have to hand a bottle of the magical, golden restorative – Irn-Bru.

And just a word about the daft idea from our Russian friend that the English are greater connoisseurs of whisky than the Scots – rubbish! Scotch whisky is still drunk widely in Scotland although, as seems to be happening in England, more and more of my mates are switching to fine malts rather than ordinary whisky. Every day more folk overseas are discovering the delights of good Scotch and long may that continue, say I.

Salut Tipple
1 Dogger View, Fraserburgh, Aberdeenshire

On hangover cures, let's hear it for the Bloody Mary – the tomatoes therein will chase the hangover blues, although personally I would never go past my granny's leek and tattie soup. That will get you bounding about like a newborn lamb in no time. And forget this nonsense about taking water in your whisky in an effort to deaden the hangover effect. Water is a menace. You can catch all sorts of things like Legionaire's disease from water. Take it straight. Be a man. Or as Neil Munro's puffer skipper Para Handy warned: 'Water's a fine, fine thing for sailing oan – neathin' better – but it's no' a drink for sailors. It rots yer boots; what'll it no' do tae yer insides.'

Tavish Spike
Sports Editor, *The Auchenblane Bugle*, Auchenblane, Stirlingshire

The Evil Weed

In the 1600s did James VI of Scotland and I of England launch the world's first anti-smoking campaign, seeking to ban the habit in enclosed public areas?

David Stuyvesant
Ash Road, Weedon, Bucks.

Yes, with the Scottish Parliament having recently banned smoking in all enclosed public areas, it would be a neat tidying up of history if we were to find that James VI had started the ball rolling 400 years earlier. It wasn't exactly like that. The Scottish situation was that in the seventeenth century a careful watch was being kept by the Privy Council, the country's ruling body, over the import of that 'infective weed callit tobacco'. However, the feeling seems to have been that there was money to be made through taxation. James himself first of all banned its import, then, finding smugglers were making a mockery of the legislation and that the country was overflowing with tobacco, imposed a heavy tax; then he tried banning it again.

There seems little doubt that James had a strong personal aversion to tobacco and did indeed spearhead a campaign to limit its use, once having declared that smoking 'makes a sooty kitchen of the inward parts'. It would be reasonable to argue that James was indeed the man behind the first anti-smoking campaign.

Bill Reekie
Senior Service Care Home, Kilsyth, North Lanarkshire

James VI did indeed single-handedly launch a campaign against smoking, having published his *Counterblaste to Tobacco* in which he argues that the herb brought about physical as well as moral corruption. Today it is the physical aspects of tobacco which concern us most and I am old enough to remember a time when there was something odd and uncool about you if you *didn't* smoke.

Sir Walter Raleigh is credited with bringing back tobacco from North America but other evidence rather suggests that it was Sir Francis Drake. Whichever one of these bold English matelots did the deed, we learn that crowds gathered in London soon after the arrival of the first tobacco from its homeland in North America to watch sea captains light up in the street and smoke a roll-up.

A man called Ralph Lane is usually given credit, or blame, depending which side of the argument you are on, for bringing the first commercial quantities of tobacco into England around 1586, having discovered, remarkably, that North American Indians used it to cure stomach pains. James VI was merciless in an anonymous attack on Lane saying that, while the 'poor, barbarous' man who brought the habit to Britain was dead, the vile habit was 'yet alive, yea, in fresh vigour'.

However, it is fortunate for the prosperity of Scotland, and Glasgow in particular, that James was unable to hold back the tobacco tide because by the 1720s, a century after his death, the city on the Clyde was importing half of all American tobacco brought into Britain, leaving her competitors, Liverpool, Bristol and Whitehaven, dragging behind.

Nicholas O. Teen
Gasper Lane, Smoky Hollow, Massachusetts, USA

Amusingly, like any of us who stand proudly on points of principle, James was on one occasion forced to bite the bullet and allow smoking. While out hunting, a shower of rain drove his company into a pigsty for shelter. To cut the stench James had 'caused a pipefull to be taken on purpose' — Ed.

Wishful Thinking?

Fifers like to call their home county 'The Kingdom'. Does the region have any sort of valid claim to this title?

Ernest Auchterlonie
Bishop's Gate, Broad Street, Dumfries

The brief answer to this question has to be 'no'. If there is to be a valid explanation of this common usage it must relate to the geography of the region. The Fife peninsula, fringed to the north by the River Tay and to the south by the Forth, is one of the most distinctive districts of Scotland.

Some would take it further. They would argue that Fife is culturally different from the rest of Scotland, having, from a very early date, been influenced by trade with the continent of Europe which has given the people a distinctively outgoing nature, unlike so many other Scottish districts which are insular (even if they are not islands) and self-interested. A strong seafaring tradition also marks out the region. Another feature which could be said to make Fife 'feel' different from the rest of Scotland, or at least the adjacent regions, is its climate. Fifers will tell you that the sun shines on Fife when Angus and the Lothians are beneath a cloudy mantle.

Maybe the most important factor of all is that Fifers do feel different. They have a sense of regional solidarity born of shared experience over many centuries. If they have a sense of being a kingdom in their own right, who are we to deny them their birthright? But wait – if Fife is a kingdom then it must have had a king. Here, we begin to struggle.

Bill Bright
Lomond View, Penicuik, Midlothian

Mr Bright has posed the question – when did Fife ever have a king that would entitle them to call themselves a kingdom? If we pass by the obvious response that Charles I, king of Great Britain and son of James VI, was born at Dunfermline in 1600, we can concentrate on the individual who for many was the undisputed 'King' of Fife – James Curran Baxter, Slim Jim Baxter, the son of a Fife miner and arguably the most gifted footballer ever produced in Scotland.

And when, you might reasonably ask, was the King of Fife crowned? Any true fan of Scottish football will unhesitatingly give you the answer to that. The year was 1967, the season after England had won the World Cup, and Jim's coronation venue was Wembley Stadium, when the cheeky Baxter teased and tormented the English world-beaters during a famous 3–2 Scottish win.

There were two defining moments in this match which gave Slim Jim the heroic status of a Wallace or a Bruce. First of all, he had the English fans baying with fury and the English players grinding their teeth with frustration when he audaciously played keepie-uppie on the halfway line as England attempted to save face. And when he cheekily stuffed the ball up his jooks it was the ultimate slap in the face for the three lions.

Sadly, Jim's later life, characterised by heavy drinking, was very much in the mould of the Stuart dynasty and had the tragic elements of that other Fifer, Charles I, executed at the block in London.

Kirk Berstane
The Photo Booth, Tesco's Supermarket,
Maryhill Road, Glasgow

Once a Knight's Enough

Whenever we see a movie of the Wars of Independence, the Scots army is portrayed as a dirty, rude and scruffy bunch of barbarians while the English force consists of noble knights in their finery on magnificent warhorses. Did Scotland ever have an 'Age of Chivalry'?

David Rowbottom
Tournament Road, Battle, Sussex

Film-makers have their own reasons for portraying the Scots as a peasant army – it all adds to the drama, the weak overcoming the strong, David giving Goliath a sair heid, that sort of thing. In fact, the Scots army was drawn from a cross-section of the ordinary people and, in that sense, was indeed a very rough-and-ready outfit.

That the Scots generally seemed to conduct themselves in a less than chivalrous way is beyond argument. They were sneaky, they ran away if the occasion demanded and they avoided a straight head-to-head whenever possible. As far as I can determine they are still at it today. For example, in 1327 Sir James Douglas and his horse troop charged through the English camp during a night raid in Northumberland, cut the guy ropes of the royal tent and brought the whole shooting match down on a teenage Edward III. Later, the young man, on his first campaign, wept in his frustration at being unable to bring the Scots to battle. This was a very ungallant, almost sneaky, attack, under cover of darkness and typical of the Scots.

It is my argument that the tactics adopted by Scots commanders, the hit-and-run guerrilla style of warfare, limited the opportunities for the practice of chivalry, courtly love and honour found in other, civilised, European nations. It is certain that the noble element in the Scottish army was, in any case, very small, perhaps no more than a couple of hundred knights.

That most Scots had other things on their mind than the strange concept of chivalry is clear by the famous Declaration of Arbroath, signed by most of the gentlemen who might have been the flower of Scottish chivalry around 1320. The Declaration, stressing that it was freedom, and freedom only, that was being pursued, explains: 'It is in truth not for glory, nor riches, nor honours that we are fighting . . .' No room there for an honour code.

So there it is, honour, common decency and fair play were never part of the game. The idea was to throw out their natural 'superiors', to cast off what the Scots laughingly called the yoke of oppression. The Age of Chivalry passed Scotland by and no one is surprised by that.

Rev. Roger Pedant
Bury St Edmunds, Suffolk

It is easy to identify the point when the practice of chivalry had to take a back seat in the Scottish Wars of Independence. In 1307 Robert Bruce took the momentous, but arguably unchivalric, decision to wage a guerrilla war against England in the quest for independence. He recognised that in orthodox pitched battle England, with its greater resources, would always have the upper hand. Bruce opted for speed, surprise and non-confrontation, including the policy of scorched earth. Apparently the Scottish nobility were none too happy with this decision. They saw it as certainly unchivalric, possibly even cowardly. The bottom line is that the tactics worked and when the Scots veered away from this approach to warfare they invariably got a duffing.

William Bartiebeith
Castle Grim, Forteith Point, Macrahanish

Mr Rowbottom has hit upon the essence of Scotland's struggle for freedom. The Scottish army was short on pomp and majesty. Chivalry was present but it was an intriguing variant of the broader European movement. The Scots allowed themselves to drift very close to what might be seen by others as cowardice and dishonour to achieve what might be called the greatest goal of all – freedom.

Professor Darf Moriarty
The Institute of Honour Studies, 14 Paragon Street, Macclesfield

Second-String Inventors

We've all heard of Logie Baird, Macadam & Co. but there is an impression that Scots were involved in almost every innovation of the past 200 years. Is this a load of hooey or can anyone tell us anything about Scotland's lesser-known inventors?

Tracy Hunt
Discovery Road, Eureka, Colorado, USA

Scots inventors in the league of Alexander Graham Bell, John Logie Baird, James Watt and so many others are known the world over but other imaginative fellow Scots have also made many less-trumpeted breakthroughs in scientific thought, as I think Tracy suspected, particularly at the height of the Industrial Revolution.

William Murdock, the Ayrshire inventor, made the premier league thanks to his development of coal gas lighting but in his early days he might have been regarded potentially as mere second division material, his only worthwhile development having been a wooden top hat! When we look at the width rather than the quality of Scots inventiveness a staggering range of achievement materialises.

Orcadians Andrew Thomson and James Drever, who emigrated to San Francisco in the late 1800s, are credited with the invention of boiler suit fasteners but much more interestingly, at least for the red-blooded heterosexual male, in the late 1800s they produced the first clasp fastening which made possible stocking suspenders.

On a completely different tack, Scotland's beheading machine was in use in Edinburgh some 200 years before the French version, the guillotine, achieved notoriety during the Revolution. The Maiden, (and this will interest the youngsters) complete with bloodstains, is the pride and joy of our National Museum in Edinburgh.

Theology student Patrick Bell invented a reaping machine but, afraid that it would be seen as too radical, conducted his experiments at night. His fears were well founded and when news leaked out he emigrated to North America to begin his ministerial career. John Broadwood from Oldhamstocks in East Lothian invented the grand piano. He developed a new piano action and built the first six-octave grand in 1794. While we're on about grand-dads, Alexander Bain, one of thirteen children and son of a Caithness farmer, is generally held to be the inventor of the grandfather-size electric clock which, in turn, led to the adoption of Greenwich Mean Time across the country.

The list, frankly, is endless. A long history of formal and family education and an enterprising and inquisitive spirit allowed the Scots to make a disproportionate impact on the development of the modern world. We should be proud of them all.

Alec Tyson
Principal, National Union of Creative Inventors,
Nutbourne, Angus

It's interesting to note how many ordinary Scots seemingly without any particular spark of imagination began to show remarkable inventiveness immediately after emigration. Whether the emigration experience had freed their enterprise or whether it was simply the busy activity in the new lands which stirred the imagination is a subject which could be debated at great length. For example, in 1885 Scots emigrant James Candlish was following his trade as a blacksmith at Rawlins in Wyoming when he built the original sheepherder's 'home on wheels' with its own built-in stove and bunk bed. The wagon enabled the sheep farmer to spend the night far out on the range. It took the tough sheep men a wee while to adjust to the innovation and abandon their longstanding practice of sleeping on the stony ground under the stars.

I've often wondered if this piece of engineering was the earliest inspiration for that great American institution the mobile home, or Winnebago.

Roland McNeish
Freedom Motor Homes, Back Street, Wishaw

The invention business was an open house for eccentrics. Thomas Chalmers, one of the most gifted men of his generation who led the breakaway by the Free Church from the Church of Scotland in 1843, wrote proudly in his correspondence of having invented a new technique for folding his coat which he thought would be of great value to the traveller.

Rev. Pardew Auchterlonie
Zion, 11111 Queensferry Road, Edinburgh

Wild About Balmoral

Why did Queen Victoria, while searching Scotland for a Highland retreat, finally select Balmoral Castle for her Scottish seat?

Foster Wright
The Palace of Fun, Woodside, Aberdeen

I have read that when the young Queen Victoria sailed to Scotland for the first time, in 1842, she wrote in her journal of the dark, brooding Scottish coastline which was so unlike the familiar more gentle contours of the south. At this point it must have seemed unlikely that she would fall in love with Scotland, but that's how it turned out.

The Queen was twenty-three and had been married for two years to Albert. The couple were very quickly hooked on the Highlands and over the next five years a plan evolved to have a Scottish home for late summer holidays.

Interestingly, Deeside was selected, it seems, as much for its healthy climate as for its marvellous scenery. The royals were plagued with bouts of rheumatism and listened attentively to their chief physician, Sir James Clark, himself a Scotsman, when he spoke of the sunny valley of the Dee with its pure air and relatively low rainfall. His own son had recovered from illness at the Deeside home of a diplomat, Sir Robert Gordon – Balmoral.

In 1848 Albert acquired the little castle but immediately planned for a new home – the castle we see today – completed in 1856. Victoria was clearly captivated by the tranquillity of the setting. She wrote in her journal that it was the sort of place to 'make one forget the world and its sad turmoil'.

Victoria's endorsement of the Highlands as a place of sanctuary and retreat, following centuries when it had been regarded as the haunt of barbarians, was an important final seal of approval in the rehabilitation of the Highlanders after their defeat at Culloden in 1746. She said she found the people chivalrous, fine and active – but, more importantly, loyal. And the landscape was no longer threatening but safe and unspoiled.

The passion for the Highlands and its tartan trappings of this, the greatest queen Britain had ever known, meant that the love of all things 'Scottish' which she fostered has endured right into the present day. Upper-class British tourists, spearheaded by the first Thomas Cook holidays, began to flock to the lochs, glens and waterfalls mentioned by Sir Walter Scott in his novels, and to the sites visited by the Queen and Albert. They have been followed by tourists from the world over. Our Highlands have been transformed by the love of a Queen.

Rev. Wilfrid Martin
Author of *Queen Victoria – True Majesty*,
Lesmahagow, Lanarkshire

We are surely indebted to the Rev. Martin for a detailed if slightly sycophantic summary of Queen Victoria's connection with Deeside. He does make it sound as if there was an inevitability about Vicky ending up at Balmoral, almost as if she was predestined to find a home there.

The evidence is very much to the contrary and, from what I've read, the Scottish climate did indeed play a major part in her decision, but scarcely in the way that the reverend gentleman describes. After she 'discovered' Scotland but was still seeking a home here, the Queen visited Ardverikie, 'an ornate, fake-medieval castle' standing on the southern shore of Loch Laggan in Inverness-shire. This beautiful spot might easily have captured her heart but, on the day she visited, the fickle Scottish weather, which treats king and commoner alike, once again changed history. For the duration of her stay the heavens opened, there was a downpour that lasted twenty-four hours and Queen Victoria was not impressed.

So the great tartan bandwagon – and the tourist money – rolled on to Balmoral and Loch Lagganside lost out – or did they?

Affleck Gray
Coulter Building, University of South Glasgow,
Pollok Shopping Centre

Man, I don't know whether it would gar' ye greet or boke or both. Victoria came to Deeside to get away from the reality of a society which was treating the common man shamefully. Working people were expendable commodities. Humanity had been lost.

And, not so many miles from where she wandered on the hills with her ghillies and sketched the majestic slopes and Albert clumsily tried to shoot stag, people had been cleared from their homes to make way for the selfsame deer. She embraced the tartan nonsense which was basically a creation of that 'Wizard of the North' Sir Walter Scott, whose greatest trick was to formulate a heavily romanticised version of the history of Scotland that bore little or no relation to reality . . . a Scotland made safe, sanitised, for the visitor.

For Victoria, as the good Rev. said, Deeside was a place where she could forget the real world. She lived in her private paradise making charitable gifts to local families and enjoying the scenery while tens of thousands of people in the great industrial city of Glasgow, the second city of the Empire, were living in conditions of utter squalor in the tenement slums. How much Victoria knew, or cared, about this we can only guess. Her journal gives us no clue. What we do know is that while Victoria couldna' wait tae get back to her annual retreat on Deeside, thousands o' Scots were abandoning their homeland weekly to seek a better life for themselves and their families in North America or Australasia.

Comrade Dan McLean
Mick McGahey House, Clartyhole Mews, Dumbarton

Slap in the Face

Why does the supposedly all-British national anthem, 'God Save the King', contain such strong, anti-Scottish sentiments?

G. B. Singer
Factory Road, Polmont, Stirlingshire

It is wrong to suggest that the famous offending verse in 'God Save the King' refers to the Scottish people in general. The composer was referring specifically to supporters of the Stuart cause, followers of Bonnie Prince Charlie who had risen against Hanoverian control or, as the lyrics say, 'rebellious Scots'. As we know, much of Lowland Scotland was agin the Jacobite Uprising.

The current debate about anthems tends to focus on the need for a stirring, widely accepted Scottish anthem which will avoid different tunes – 'Scotland the Brave' and 'Flower of Scotland' most notably – being played at different sporting events as our national anthem. A confusing situation not only for Scots, I fear. We should realise that when one of the most important products we offer the international community is Scotland herself, through our vital tourist industry, then our image must be crystal clear.

This leads me to the 'British national anthem'. It's worth pointing out before we come over all Bruce-and-Wallace that

'God Save the King' has been, over the years, both musically and politically, all things to all people. It has been an all-purpose anthem adapted a dozen or more times by nations such as Liechtenstein and the United States for their own loyalist purposes and the words have regularly been changed or a verse added.

It is, of course, also beloved by English football fans and, more mysteriously, by Rangers supporters, who are, of course, the most loyal of the loyal, but to what, they're not quite sure.

It was the addition of a verse, when General Wade set out for Scotland with his army on 6 October 1745 for the campaign that ended in the field of Culloden, that has given offence to so many Scots over the years. The new verse ran:

> Lord grant that Marshal Wade
> May, by thy might aid,
> Victory bring.
> May he sedition hush,
> And like a torrent rush,
> Rebellious Scots to crush –
> God save the King.

Interestingly, the melody of 'God Save the King' was popular with both Jacobites and Hanoverians – as I say, an all-purpose anthem. I suppose a useful comparison might be the way in which Lily Marlene was claimed by both the Eighth Army and the Afrika Corps during World War II. My own choice – if pressed – would be for 'Amazing Grace' which never fails to stir the emotions.

Peter Tyson
Author of *Gie's a Song – a History of Anthems*,
Billaricay, Essex

I really don't know why, as Scots, we should be asked to sing the national anthem of our oppressive English neighbours. The reason, Mr Singer, that 'God Save the King or Queen' still has any credibility at all (with or without the anti-Scottish verse) is that in our very Scottish way we have been unable to agree amongst ourselves on the best Scottish anthem to replace the imperialist dirge that is 'God Save the King'. Let's be done with all the bickering and agree that 'Donald, Whaur's Yer Troosers?' summarises the dignity and pride in nation which characterises the Scots. Let this song be our greeting to the world.

Holden McGroyne
The Music Schule, Peebles Place, San Bernadino,
California, USA

A Questionable Gift

We often hear it said that Highland Scots have a psychic gift, a special ability to see into the future, which has been dubbed 'second sight'. If this is true, why didn't they see Culloden coming?

Ed Case
Karmic Way, Wishaw, Lanarkshire

It's pretty clear from the low, facetious tone of Mr Case's inquiry that he is sceptical that the gift of second sight is a reality. Let me assure him that it has existed for thousands of years and is a real and present force in our community to this day. To emphasise my point I would suggest very strongly that Mr Case reconsider the little jaunt to Tenerife that he's planning for next month and in particular the need to take an attractive young lady from his typing pool, Mags McGlone, along to help him with the 'filing'. Frankly, I don't think your marriage will stand the strain, Ed Case, you rascal. As to the failure to anticipate Culloden, it is clear that Mr Case lacks the spiritual nous to see that we all have a role to act out in life. Seeing into the future does not allow us to flee from our responsibilities but gives us the opportunity to face up to our destiny with fortitude and serenity. Call this Calvinist predestination if you like but I would only say that the old Kirk didn't get everything wrong.

Claire Voyans
'The Monklands Seer', The Old Curiosity Shop,
Coatbridge

Ignoring completely the tongue-in-cheek inquiry (it's in the same mould as the newspaper headline: 'Fortune Telling Seminar Cancelled Due to Unforeseen Circumstances') from the doubtful Mr Bangor it's worth stressing that some fascinating new insights have been emerging in recent years about the nature of second sight, its origins and its characteristics.

Second sight is a form of clairvoyance (seeing objects not actually present to the sense of sight) but relates specifically to the historic ability of people, particularly in the Western Highlands and Islands, to glimpse future events, either directly or in symbolic form. This includes, most famously and ominously, seeing the imminent death of family and friends. The stories resulting from episodes of second sight are numerous but generally focus on the fundamental rites of passage, birth, life and death, the latter being most numerous and dramatic. In the modern setting, one Edinburgh researcher cited the case of a Highland bus driver who had a vision of a funeral procession while he was behind the wheel. By recognising the mourners he was able to tell his passengers the name of the person who would die. This is very typical.

It is now thought possible that the 'gift' of prophetic vision, reports of which date back three centuries and are woven into the tapestry of Scottish oral tradition, may, in fact, be hereditary. Even more interesting is the growing body of evidence that second sight is not just restricted to the Western Isles and the Highlands but surveys are showing that the phenomenon occurs all over Scotland.

If the truth is that clairvoyance, including second sight, is more often reported in the Celtic homelands, this could well be because the Celts are traditionally 'dreamers' and more open-minded to the possibility of 'supernatural' episodes. The Anglo-Saxon peoples by contrast tend to be more aggressive and pragmatic, and the 'clairvoyant faculties', which they may have once shared with their Celtic neighbours, have been suppressed. In short, they have forgotten how to set their imagination free.

Professor Al B. Jenzian
Dept of Celtic Mysteries, University of the Montana Highlands, Butte, USA

Shrinking Violets?

To her dying day, my mother, originally from Forfar, always insisted that Scots were naturally a shy and usually introverted people. Is this still the case?

Patrick Meek
Peaceful Pastures, Manitoba, Canada

I wonder on which planet Mr Meek's mother was living. The Scots are the most exuberant, expressive, self-assured people I have ever met. However, I should point out that my encounters with them have been as a referee or linesman at European soccer matches over the past twenty years. Invariably before and after the game they want to talk to you. Language never seems to be a problem; they can make themselves understood in a whole range of non-verbal ways. Shy – the Scots? I don't think so.

Señor Rafael Martinez
Calle Railway, 7-Bl, Sevilla, Spain

You wouldn't think it to see the demonstrative rugby and football fans but Scots are indeed, as Mr Meek's mum suggested, basically a shy race: social anxiety is much more widespread than we care to admit. The roots of Scottish shyness run deep into the culture. If you're the sort of person who at social gatherings has the uncomfortable feeling that there are not enough corners in the room where you can hide, then don't despair – you are simply following your natural Calvinistic bent. Scots are still, rightly to my mind, held to be particularly prone to shyness, most probably because of our religious, intellectual and social history, which basically amounted to being oppressed or repressed or both.

The fact that we are making some sort of 'progress' with self-assertion here in Scotland is surely evidenced by the fact that you are unlikely to have encountered a shy, retiring estate agent, insurance or car salesman, advertising agent, or tanning centre operative. Self-confidence, assurance, is spreading like the plague through our society. People are beginning to believe in themselves and are not afraid to let the world know about it. It is fast becoming a prerequisite of living a normal life in this complex, competitive world.

The old Scots saying, 'Yer fair away wi' yersel the noo; but believe me, you'll pay for it,' is now discredited. The meek may eventually inherit the earth, as we're promised, but it won't be for the next wee while.

For the shy legions in this assertive society, problems escalate. You've seen them many times before. They can spend half an hour at a crowded bar trying to lay down an order for a drink; they encounter basically the same problem at the counters of large department stores, supermarket checkouts and in bank queues. And they never, ever do themselves justice in interviews simply because they are too strung up and hyper.

The very nature of their problem means that the 'shies' never step forward to put their case for better understanding. They are left to make insignificant little gestures to bank tellers, buroo staff, perhaps scowling meaningfully before reverting to type and finding it necessary to apologise, sucking on their teeth, struggling for words, wishing the floor would swallow them up. No, the Scottish cringe remains real enough. Oh, that we could all bare our erses in the centre of European capitals. Sadly, the world doesn't work that way and, to be truthful, most of us really shouldn't be baring anything.

Two interesting examples of the shy Scottish character – Nessie, the Loch Ness monster, who, for a thousand years, has failed to put in a conclusive appearance; that she exists is beyond dispute but despite being a monster clearly lacks self-confidence. Earl Haig of Bemersyde, commander of British forces in World War I, was so shy he never addressed his troops.

The Scots are generally shy. That's for sure – and what else would you expect in a nation where for 400 years children were told that they should be seen and not heard? Perhaps surprisingly, I find the largest proportion of shyness among the young and the middle aged. They are unquestionably the worst offenders, always hanging back and mumbling when self-assurance is what's needed. It is also worth noting that this shyness is seldom found south of the Border. The mobile, independent elderly are the social grouping in Scotland who seem to have shrugged off shyness most effectively. Sweet little old ladies are hard to find – they are more likely to be shoving their bus concession pass under some poor driver's nose or haranguing some innocent traffic warden.

Bertha Cannon
Author of *Shy Society – a Study of the Modest Scot*,
Humbie, East Lothian

Sword Swallower

Our class is re-enacting the Battle of Culloden for our school pageant and we want to make it as realistic as possible. Does anyone know where I can lay my hands on a claymore?

Caris O'Conner
Primary VI, Auchenblane School, Stirlingshire

First of all, it's a bit of a mystery to me why Scottish schoolchildren should be asked to replay one of the most punishing defeats suffered by the Scots in our long history of warfare. What are your teachers thinking about? Wouldn't a nature ramble on Loch Lomondside, an outing to New Lanark, a visit to the Glasgow Science Centre or a reconstruction of the Battle of Stirling Bridge be much more constructive and rewarding?

Assuming for a minute that you are determined to press ahead with your project, Caris, then the first thing you have to get correct is the terminology. The sword you are seeking is not the claymore, which was a huge weapon of the Middle Ages with a blade sometimes over six feet in length. In every sense this was a unique weapon. For one thing it was the largest battle sword that we know of – the only sword of equivalent size was found in medieval times in the German states – where it was an instrument of the executioner's trade. The claidh mhor, which seems to have been a weapon favoured by Highlanders and Islemen, was too long to be carried at the hip and so it was carried vertically, along the line of the bearer's spine. The hilt would project over the head and the sword was drawn for action by dragging it forwards and upwards. I suspect this had to be done with great care. It would be swung in a circular motion above the head and four warriors each using a claymore and strategically placed might protect the monarch and the royal standard in battle by creating a deadly four-pointed reaper.

The weapon used at Culloden in the 1700s, and surely the one you are seeking, would probably have been the basket-handled sword, which is an altogether lighter and more versatile piece of fighting equipment, occasionally with an intricately worked hand guard.

There are sword manufacturers in different parts of Scotland making replica swords (try the Yellow Pages) but frankly, I think you should be suggesting to your woodwork teacher (if such a creature still exists in the modern school) that he (or she) knock off a few wooden basket-handled swords for your re-enactment.

Dr Edwin Sharp
Dept of Scottish History, University of Life, Lesmahagow

All A-Flutter

Can the Lord Lyon King of Arms stop my mother flying the Saltire in her own back garden?

Theresa Forbes
Flagstaff, Arizona, USA

Surprisingly it's not the Lord Lyon – guardian of all things armorial and heraldic in Scotland – you should be worrying about, Theresa. His main concern is with the yellow and red Lion Rampant, which is the personal banner of the King or Queen of Scots. Under laws dating back to 1672, use of the Lion Rampant without Crown permission is an offence punishable – according to some wags – by beheading. Only a handful of cases relating to the Lion Rampant have ever been prosecuted in the past twenty-five years. Apparently a strongly worded warning letter usually suffices. The actual penalty, rather than losing your napper, is a fine of £100. I'm guessing that prosecution of the Tartan Army for regularly flaunting the Lion Rampant regulations on the terraces is unlikely.

Harry Herald
Shields Road, Glasgow

The Saltire is, of course, the people's flag – and we are the peepel! So your mum should fly it with pride – but, please bear in mind, planning authorities throughout Scotland might be watching you. If your pole is offensively large then you're in trouble. Surprisingly, and annoyingly, in England and Wales the Town and Country Planning Act allows automatic planning permission for flagpoles flying the St George's Cross, as anyone passing through that green and pleasant land would have noticed during the World Cup in June 2006. After devolution I understand some Scots keen to display their patriotism decided against buying a flagpole when it was pointed out that planning permission might be needed.

However, despite restrictions there are Saltires around and it is clear that enlightened authorities must be turning a blind eye to this outrageously patriotic behaviour. Although they must worry about a rash of flagpoles across the land, government at local and national level is currently more concerned about the forests of wind generators which are coming from Dunsinane to a hillside near you.

Arthur King
Tolmace, Castle Street, Dumbarton

Flying national flags on front lawns and from byre roofs in places like Scandinavia, France and the United States is commonplace, as I'm sure you'll know, Theresa. Interestingly the Saltire, or St Andrew's Cross, is claimed as the oldest national flag in Europe and was adopted by William the Lyon as early as 1165. It seems only right and proper that, with that sort of pedigree, the Saltire should be fluttering freely throughout Scotland.

The Honourable Ross Snowdon-Marchmont
Albany, Islay Road, Rothesay

Fun, Fun, Fun

Can anyone tell me anything about the history of April Fool's Day spoofs in Scotland and perhaps some of the more interesting jests that have been played?

Cherry Stones
Milngavie, by Glasgow

Am I getting old or has a lot of the innocent fun gone out of April Fool's Day in Scotland? I'm in my eighties now but I can remember as we went to school between the wars going up to some unsuspecting adult on 1 April and saying: 'You've got soot on your nose.' When the victim made to rub the soot off we would cheer – 'Hint-a-gock!' – and run off. Or we might approach a grown-up in the street and tell them that they had just dropped a pound note (now sadly gone forever) and when they turned to begin the search up would go the cry again of 'hint-a-gock'. If we were being truly outrageous we might tell a man that his zip was open.

Nowadays, for an April Fool's joke to be successful it seems it must be complex to the point where often the actual joke is lost or, alternatively, must involve activity which to my mind is nothing short of vandalism. The destruction of, or damage to, property seems to form an essential part of any worthwhile April Fool's prank these days.

For what it's worth, my favourite of all time was the famous David Dimbleby 'Spaghetti Harvest' spoof on the BBC in 1957. So many people, including myself, were taken in by the authentic voice of the Beeb telling us that pasta grew on trees. It was amazing. I still chuckle at the thought of having fallen for it, hook, line and sinker.

Diamond Rigg
Back of Beyond Old Folks' Home, Parsley End, Worcs.

Shy, retiring old people like myself live in dread of April Fool's Day and the terrible tricks that may be played on one by those obnoxious children from next door. On that theme, did you know that this fear of 1 April jests is a recognised illness and has been dubbed 'Aphrilophobia'?

Bill Andben
Halfway Up, The Rest and Be Thankful, Argyll

Scotland has a unique place in the annals of the April Fool's joke. I know this, Cherry, because I am involved in serious study of all interesting Scottish traditions. I do this so that I might more easily settle in my new home in the north. Whereas the miserly English tradition insists that all jokes must cease at midday on 1 April, Scotland continues her celebrations, or at least did for many years, into a second day.

April Fool's Day was followed in many parts of Scotland by 'taily-day' when you might suddenly be conscious that everyone was pointing at you and laughing – would screw your head round to find a paper tail had been pinned to the bottom of your jacket. In fact the whole day seemed to be a sort of cult of the posterior.

There are many theories about the origins of April Fool's Day. The silliness may have originated in France with the Poisson d'Avril or 'April Fish' and represents the change to the Gregorian calendar when New Year was moved to 1 January from the end of March. Romans and druids also get the blame but my favourite theory concerns the dove sent out by Noah to find land as the waters of the Great Flood began to subside. The dove returned on 1 April and told Noah: 'There's land out there right enough, boss.' Every creature strains to catch sight of dry land but the dove waits for his moment and triumphantly shouts: 'April Fool!'

The greatest Scottish April Fool's joke surely came in the 1920s when a female swimmer was greeted at the Broomielaw apparently having swum the Atlantic. The spoof, which drew a vast, unwitting crowd of 40,000 people, was organised by Charles Oakley, who was in later years to become a noted authority on the history of Glasgow.

Prince Barker ben Adhem
Castle Notorious, Top o' the Glen Estate, Wester Ross

His Highness Prince Barker may know a bit about the history of April Fool's Day but he has screwed up badly on the famous 'transatlantic swim'. This was not an April Fool but the greatest-ever stunt organised by Glasgow Students Charities Day Committee. Had it been on 1 April it would indeed have qualified as the nation's most spectacular April Fool.

Proudfoot Fish
Senior Pool Attendant, Stormay Public Baths, Orkney

Cats and Dogs Next?

I am compiling a register of unusual objects which have fallen from the skies over Scotland. Can anyone help?

Frederick Dailly
Callander, Perthshire

The occurrence I have to offer must surely be what we term today an urban myth but the details are so specific I just wonder. Apparently on 8 January 1846, the *Inverness Courier*, a paper of repute here in the north, reported how a flock of pigeons flew over a house belonging to a gentleman in Lochcarron. The man managed to get a shot away as they passed, hitting one of the birds. It dropped straight down the chimney into a pot of soup which was simmering over the fire. Now that takes a bit of believing, doesn't it? You see what I mean about urban myths? In passing it also occurs to me we may have, in this story, whether it is accurate or a fabrication, the origins of the phrase 'one for the pot'. Whatever the truth of this report, it can surely be termed 'an unusual fall'.

Baxter Du Cott
Glen of the Eagle, Ross-shire

There are reports of objects falling out of the skies of Scotland throughout the centuries, and not just leaves from the trees or our feathered friends. Sadly, the majority of the older stories are difficult to verify. However, I can give two fairly modern examples, one more easily explained than the other. Fish falls have been recorded in various parts of Scotland. One of the best-documented incidents was in Campbeltown, Argyll, in 1904 when a loud pattering on the roofs of houses brought people into the street to find that a shower of hundreds of small fish was falling. Half a century later – in January 1951 – a block of ice from a passing aircraft crashed through the roof of a joiner's shop in Dumbarton Road, Glasgow. This was identified as having dropped from the toilet of a passing aircraft. Similar falls have been reported all over Britain. As for the fish, the most widely held explanation for this phenomenon is that waterspouts suck fish from the water and deposit them miles away. I am struggling to find any record of it ever having rained cats and dogs in Scotland. The only way you can be sure this is happening is by going outside and finding yourself stepping in a poodle!

Foder Merrick
Dunvegan, Skye

I was intrigued by Mr Merrick's stories of fish falls and lumps of ice plunging out the sky. Snow and hail storms are common enough in Scotland and occasionally these can be spectacular. In 1807, as a violent hailstorm pounded Glasgow, one piece of ice which fell in a Duke Street backcourt was five inches by four. But that was nothing compared with a remarkable event in January 1849. Long before aircraft toilets were dropping ice blocks, *The Times of London* reported that, after an extraordinary peal of thunder, an irregular-shaped mass of ice fell on a Ross-shire estate. This, if we can believe the despatches, was no ordinary hailstone. It was said to be twenty feet in circumference! This tumbling iceberg stretches credibility a little!

Other interesting falls include an event in 1650 when, over a three-mile stretch of Lord Buccleuch's estate near the English border, it 'rained blood'. This odd phenomenon has been explained more recently by meteorologists as rain discoloured by sand blown north from the Sahara. In roughly the same period, odd reports from Clydesdale described pikes and muskets falling from some unlikely armoury in the sky. Such reports often coincide with periods of religious unrest. My own candidate for the most unlikely object to come out of the skies – certainly in the twentieth century – must be Adolf Hitler's deputy Rudolf Hess who, in 1941, landed by parachute in a field at Eaglesham in Renfrewshire, in an apparent attempt to negotiate peace.

Midge Montgomery (Ms)
The Shelter, Walthamstow

6

Mountain and glen

Invasion of the Bloodsuckers

Why is the midge such a feared creature in your country? Has anyone ever been killed in an attack by Highland midges? For that matter, does anyone like midges?

Edgar B. Cafard
Avenue des Moucherons, 33366 Montpellier, France

Not really something to joke about this because the very thought of being overwhelmed by a cloud of midges is enough to send some folk into hysterics. What might terrify midgophobes is the revelation that there are 137 varieties of the beastie throughout the world, thirty-three of which are found in Scotland, and a normal birth produces 100 extra little biters.

Most dreaded of all is the Highland midge (*Culicoides impunctatus* to give it its Sunday name) which is exceptionally large – smaller than its cousin the mosquito but vicious with it. The Lowland midge is a wimp alongside this predator.

There is an unsourced story of how some clan chieftains would have wrongdoers tied to a stake near the edge of a loch at dusk and left to the mercy of the dark swarms of midges. Madness from this excruciating torture was apparently not unknown, death not unheard of. Less terminally, the midge has sent campers, bowlers, athletes, shinty players, golfers and tourists scurrying for cover over the years. In the forests during the summer, midges regularly force timbermen to abandon work. Up to 20 per cent of production can be lost in this way.

The startling thing about the midge is that it appears to have absolutely no redeeming or endearing features. I am not an overly religious person but I do wonder what God was doing the day he created midges. It must have, as we say, been a bad day at the office. You can only think that they were placed on earth in order to provide scientists with the challenge of finding the best way to kill them.

There is also a very chauvinistic element in this problem because, like the mosquito, only the female midge bites; and although they prefer the blood of dogs, rabbits, deer and cattle they will take human blood (as long as you don't wave your arms around hysterically and disturb their feeding). Scientists believe that if the instinct for pairing can be restrained then the swarming would not take place. Decoding the chemical messages which the females send out may offer the solution. Like most problems in life, sex seems to be the source of the problem.

Sam Moss
Quito, Ecuador

One person who knew a bit about midges was Neil Munro's Para Handy. He does not record any deaths from midge attack but Para Handy was convinced that in different parts of the West of Scotland the midge tribes displayed different characteristics. For example he declares:

> Look at Tignabruigh. They're that bad there,
> they'll bite their way through corrugated iron

> to get at you. Take Clynder or any other place
> on the Gareloch you'll see the old ones leading
> the young ones, learning them the proper
> grips.

Cures for the midge over the years are spectacularly varied and have included dousing yourself in paraffin or whisky or leaving Danish blue cheese around to act as a diversion.

Historically, there is absolutely no doubt that the midge was a menace. One theory has it that the retreat of the Roman legions can be laid at the midge's door. Robert Bruce and his freedom fighters suffered from their attentions in the fourteenth century and Queen Victoria is reputed to have allowed gentlemen to smoke at Balmoral to keep the midge at bay.

Writer Alan Kidd describes how midges caused cricket matches to be cancelled, harassed picnics held by the Royal Family and, on one famous occasion, a goalkeeper during a match at Fort William running from his line after being attacked by midges only to see a long shot from an observant forward hit the back of the net.

In his letter Mr Moss suggests that there is no purpose to the life of the midge but in this he is totally wrong. If you've ever watched birds or bats along the West Coast diving into these legions of midges then you'll know that they are enjoying a hearty meal. God does have a plan, you see, and the midge has its part to play. Even the diabolical horsefly and the cleg are there for a purpose. Truly, what a wonderful world we inhabit.

Rev. Grant Tulloch
Church of Transforming Miracles, Glasgow Road,
Clydebank

A million and one cures have been suggested to rid yourself of midges but it may be that if you stink properly then the wee blighters are no problem. Scientists at Aberdeen, I read, have discovered that of the 400 or so chemicals which issue from our skin (a frightening thought in itself) several are detested by midges. Seems it's just your luck if you stink correctly. The boffins are now trying to develop a new natural repellent from the key chemicals.

Arthur P. Rank
The Shambles, Hawick, The Borders

I like midges! I really do! As Europe's premier masticater of live insects (currently appearing at the Casino, Bridlington), I can tell you that the midge, lightly spread on an oatcake, is a rare delicacy. It is the entomological equivalent of caviar – a rare treat. Its slightly bitter aftertaste, to my mind, simply adds to the piquancy to the dish. Scotland may be missing an opportunity to lead the way here in marketing midge paste which I feel would be popular in South East Asia – while at the same time ridding itself of a nuisance. Put me down for a jar, anyway.

Paul Proboscis
The Hive, Anthill, Surrey

Gie Them a Blaw!

Recently I read with disbelief that the Scots did not invent the bagpipes. More than that, my college friend Eugene also says that, in the mid 1700s, the Scots abandoned the pipes altogether and instead started to concentrate on the fiddle.

Donald Drone
Wind River Technical College, Bloustery, Utah, USA

The invention of the bagpipe is variously attributed to the Chinese, the Romans and, just occasionally, to the Scots, Donald. Along with the drum, harp and flute, it is unquestionably an ancient instrument and may have developed independently in different parts of the world. The first representation of the bagpipe is found on a weathered Hittite carving of the thirteenth century BC.

The bagpipe was popular in Rome and described by the historian Suetonius as 'the instrument of war of the Roman infantry'. There seems a distinct possibility that it was the Roman legionaries – who, of course, spent time in Scotland trying, among other things, to keep warm – who brought the pipes to the hills and glens of Scotland.

What is not in dispute is that it was in Scotland and, in particular, the Highlands, an area cut off from mainstream European culture, that the bagpipe flourished as other gentler instruments became popular elsewhere in Europe. Its strident tone made it the supreme outdoor instrument and, by the later Middle Ages, pipe tunes echoing along the glens had become a sound as distinctively Scottish as the cry of the curlew.

I suspect that your friend, in making reference to the Scots shunning the pipes sometime in the 1700s, must be thinking of the post-Culloden crackdown on everything associated with Highland culture, the 'dark age' as some of us call it, when the carrying of arms, the wearing of the kilt, the language and the bagpipe were proscribed. As in Roman times the bagpipe was deemed to be an instrument of war and, for thirty-two years, it was outlawed.

Incidentally, piping at this period has it very own martyr – in 1746 piper James Reid was accused at York of being in possession of arms, a bagpipe. A defiant Jacobite, Reid was hanged. It is true that, during this period, the fiddle probably was widely used but it had always been a popular instrument with the ordinary folk.

Ned Culver
Pipe Major, The Wee Mental Blowhards of Cincinnati Pipe Band, Ohio, USA

It is difficult for non-Scots to appreciate just how important the bagpipe is to Caledonian culture. Whatever its origins, it was in the mountains of Scotland that it prospered and was nurtured.

Properly played, the bagpipe can express grief, rapture or courage. And it is not, as the pseudo-intellectuals might try to tell you, something that has been foisted on the Scottish people as some sort of phoney icon. It is built into the culture. There is a great love of the bagpipes among Highlanders and Lowlanders alike and whatever the tune, the bagpipe is arguably the most potent symbol of Scotland and the Scottish heritage.

In the Stratford district of Taranaki, New Zealand, I remember, the arrival of the telephone helped one of my recently arrived immigrant neighbours, a fellow Scot, to cure serious homesick blues. When she began to feel low, particularly at weekends, she would pick up the phone and call a Scots friend locally who then played the pipes to her over the phone – much to the disgust of the other twenty people on the party line.

James 'Happy' McAllister
Funeral Director, End of the Road,
Wellington, New Zealand

Death Rays and Soap Operas

While on holiday our guide told us a little about your so-called vitrified forts which seem very mysterious. What exactly are they and can you also say why they are found only in Scotland?

Donahue Tag
Scatsbury Cove, Massachusetts, USA

You are correct, Mr Tag, in describing these forts as mysterious. They represent one of the great, as yet unresolved, riddles of Scottish archaeology. Scattered across Scotland from the Solway Firth in the south up and across to Aberdeenshire and then across to the Western Isles, these Iron Age hilltop constructions are roughly circular with massive walls made from piled stones. Here the puzzle unfolds. The rocks have at some point in their archaeological history been subjected to an intense heat, over 1,000°C, say the experts, sufficient to turn them molten. On cooling they become a glass-like – 'vitrified' – solid.

Earliest scientific studies in the 1700s suggested they had been built from volcanic rock but this has now been proved to be incorrect. It is now clear that they were fired after construction (either deliberately or accidentally), heavy interlacing timbers in the wall helping to build up a fearsome heat in the heart of the rocks. Several schools of thought – some of the fruit-and-nut variety – exist in relation to the origins of these forts. Some believe they were deliberately fired to strengthen them or make them impervious to water but the most likely explanation is that they were set alight by besieging forces.

Why are they only found in Scotland? This is probably the greatest mystery of all because hilltop forts are characteristic of Celtic Europe and have been found in Germany, Scandinavia and Ireland. However, none of these sites show any evidence of vitrification.

Professor I. N. Ferno
College of Great World Mysteries,
Harbour Road, Bellshill, Lanarkshire

The absence of detailed research studies into the nature of hill forts points to a government cover-up. Members of Alien Outreach (Inverurie Branch) are convinced that vitrified forts represent evidence of an attempt by an extraterrestrial civilisation to take over Scotland during the Iron Age.

Anyone visiting the hill fort on top of Bennachie will know that no known human technology could have fired up the ramparts to such a heat as to fuse them into a glassy mass of stones. This is clearly the work of an advanced civilisation who were intent on putting down the wild Pictish natives of the country where they had chosen to settle. They would have used what cheap newspapers might call a 'death ray' to literally melt the Pictish defences.

It seems quite possible that these alien peoples are still amongst us here in Scotland but have abandoned the technique of turning fortresses to stone and adopted instead a policy of vitrifying people by posing as BBC scriptwriters and forcing them to watch episodes of *River City*.

Andromeda Stark
The Steading, by Alford, Aberdeenshire

No Tea Bags Required

I was distressed when visiting Scotland last year on a shooting expedition to discover that in several locations the domestic water supply was brown. When I inquired with our bus driver Luigi, I was told, 'It's just poor Pete.' Can someone explain Pete's problem?

Roland Patrice
Piazza Clemente, Bologna, Italy

While studying in Minnesota one of my lecturers used to ask his students, 'What's brown, foams, preserves bodies for thousands of year, yet is safe enough to drink?'

The answer is, of course, peat-stained water. That is what you encountered in Scotland. The colour comes from tannic acid found in incompletely decomposed vegetation. It has a tea-like flavour when boiled and the tannin has numerous preservative and medicinal properties. Oh yes, the bodies! Its preservative qualities are best shown by the hundreds of North European 'bog bodies' dating from the Iron Age, often sacrificial victims, which are found preserved in peat.

Oscar Rubric
Boghead Road, Dumbarton

The English language can sometimes prove quite mystifying to Johnny foreigner.

Here, however, is a simple misunderstanding. What your bus driver was trying to say was that in many parts of Scotland the water is stained by the peaty soil, adding a special piquancy not only to the water but also to the malt whisky manufactured from it. He was, I think, saying: 'It's just pure peat.' It's an easy mistake for anyone learning English/Scottish to make.

Peaches Cavendish
Language Assistant, Tranent College of Medieval Tongues, East Lothian

For many Victorians hunters, stalkers, walkers and holiday-makers the prospect of a soak in a bathful of peaty brown water after a day on the hills was akin to a religious experience. In the last decade a number of attempts have been made to rid Highland water of its rich brown character, all in the name of public order, political correctness and standardisation. However, latest field reports suggest that the uniformity police are finding it difficult to break the peat habit.

It is also ironic that the Highlands should be split over what colour of water might be most appropriate in the twenty-first century at a time when a permanent drought appears to have settled over the south-east of England.

Now I'm sure Signor Patrice would be interested to have an assessment of the risks he runs in coming into contact with 'poor Pete'. When dried, peat provides an aromatic, if hazy, warmth. And although bathing in peaty water seems at first to be akin to swimming in sewage, remember the peat is as old as the hills it springs from and, if analysed, would probably be much purer than anything coming from a London tap.

Alastair Robertson once wrote that for the English upper middle classes and their Scottish cousins, 'peaty water is the one sure sign that they have escaped into a true wilderness where not even the long arm of European purifying legislation can reach.' Perhaps we shouldn't be so sure of that.

There is, of course, a problem for those who drink whisky on the rocks, or gin and tonic. Dark brown ice cubes take a bit of getting used to.

Edwin Marsh
The National Association of Peat Water Dippers, Bath, Somerset

◎ Edinburgh's Lost Loch

Imelda, my dear wife of fifty years, and I are planning a trip to Edinburgh and we have read of your capital's famous Nor' Loch. We imagine it must be very picturesque, lying so near the city center. Sadly, we can't find it on any of the maps available here in Idaho or on the holiday leaflets we have collected. Can anyone help?

Mac Schwimmer
Lakeside, Idaho

Mr Schwimmer shouldn't worry about finding the Nor' Loch. If he takes a train trip from the city he will leave Edinburgh along what was formerly the bed of the Nor' Loch. As the name suggests, it lay on the northern flank of the castle rock and after being drained in the nineteenth century, Waverley Station and Princes Street Gardens were laid out on the site, where they remain to this day.

The history of this vanished Edinburgh landmark is intriguing. It was a man-made loch created on the orders of the Stuart kings in the 1400s. It filled a vast trough left by the ice sheet as it flowed around the Castle Rock, which is, in fact, a hard volcanic plug. On the other side of the rock the Cowgate was formed in the same manner by the southern branching of the ice.

Doug Dipper
Deep End, Melrose

The Nor' Loch was an artificial stretch of water below the northern ramparts of the castle and formed an important part of the defence of the old town of Edinburgh which had grown out along the ridge below Castle Rock. Like much of the land around the castle and its ridge, the area of the Nor'

Loch was marshy. French visitors to Edinburgh in the later Middle Ages saw a city almost surrounded by the water of these swamps, so much so that you occasionally see references in correspondence to Edinburgh as L'Isleburg.

It seems that for a time the Nor' Loch was a very picturesque spot but it became overgrown and filled with the sewage and the waste produce of the medieval city and became, effectively, a stagnant cesspit. Despite this contamination it appears still to have been used as a source of water. It is also reported to have become a popular place for would-be suicides, it provided access to the city for smugglers and is also thought to have been a site for punishment.

Naturally, it was also a very attractive location for adventurous children, especially when frozen over in winter. There are regular reports of fatal accidents in and around the loch. In 1655 the Nor' Loch found its way into the annals for a rather bizarre reason. An exceptionally fierce storm cast up thousands of eels on its banks.

Jack 'Swampy' Montrose
Mangrove Terrace, Lochgelly, Fife

The Nor' Loch was, as previous correspondents have indicated, on the present site of Waverley Station. What has not been made sufficiently clear is that its infilling was not a single event but went on over many years. First of all it was much reduced by draining during the construction of the North Bridge and then it was divided in two by the construction of the Mound to link the Old and New Towns of Edinburgh. By this time the end of the Nor' Loch was in sight. My own view is that a recreated Nor' Loch on that location would enhance the southern prospect from Princes Street which is already the most magnificent city centre view in Europe. The future is with the internal combustion engine and not the railways. Who needs Waverley after all? Bring back the Nor' Loch, say I.

Michael Partridge
Hemel Hempstead, Herts.

I have enjoyed the flurry of letters seeking to help Mr Schwimmer of Idaho with his upcoming visit to Scotland but a very important aspect of the history of the Nor' Loch has been omitted. The noxious story of the loch mentioned by one correspondent – smugglers, suicides, etc. – is only part of it. For many years this sinister and filthy pool was used as the site for testing supposed witches to determine their guilt – if they floated they were guilty, if they drowned they were innocent.

Above the site of the loch on the Castle Hill, many of my sister white witches were burned at the stake, innocents who never dabbled in the black arts and whose only crime was that they were lonely individualists who tried to help others in an age of fear and superstition.

If you ask me, the eradication of this foul and malignant stretch of water was no loss.

Abigail Dispenser
Bespoke Broomsticks, Yon Creepy Way,
Ipswich, Norfolk

◉ Wing and a Prayer

Scotland has many symbols – the bagpipe, the kilt, the ginger 'See You Jimmy' bunnet – but I would argue that the golden eagle is our nation's most potent icon. Is the golden eagle now truly a rare species and where are the best locations in Scotland to see the bird in its natural setting?

Francis Feather

Treetops, Port Glasgow, Renfrewshire

I think very few would argue that the golden eagle, with its magnificent wingspan of up to two metres and a cruising speed of 80 mph, is a precious emblem of wild Scotland, representing as it does individuality, freedom and lonely places. However, the modern world touches these birds even in their remote eyries.

Almost all the breeding golden eagles in Britain are to be found north of the Border. One report I saw suggested that there were 440 pairs, with the most impressive growth in numbers being in the Hebrides, while a decline has been noted on the mainland. Grampian has only eighteen breeding pairs and the loss of a bird on Royal Deeside in the summer of 2006 through poisoning provoked familiar arguments between the hunting lobby and the conservationists. The fact is that these birds are under threat of poisoning or shooting in the East and South of Scotland if they hunt over the lucrative grouse moors, and they have also lost many of the open, treeless areas in the West of Scotland, which they favour, to forestry development.

We cannot expect these splendid birds ever to be widely found. They occasionally have hunting territories which can extend to 150 square kilometres but they are unquestionably very sensitive to human disturbance. They do not migrate and remain in their breeding areas all year round, hunting for small birds, snakes, grouse and hare.

You ask about locations where they are likely to be seen. You have a chance of seeing this majestic bird soaring on the thermals in a number of places throughout Scotland including Glen Affric in Inverness-shire, the Kilmichael Forest in Argyll, Portree in Skye, the Great Glen Forest, Crinan, Carradale, Raasay and the Knapdale Forest.

Samuel Dove
Editor of *Feathered Scotland*, Swallow Road,
Faifley, Clydebank, West Dunbartonshire

Whaur's the Bloomin' Heather?

Can it be true that Scotland's heather moorlands are fast disappearing?

Patrick Heath
Smokehouse No. 4, The Promenade, Arbroath, Angus

Heather had many uses in Highland cottages up to the twentieth century. It was utilised in bedding, in thatching, as firewood, to make ale, tea, medicines, dye, baskets, brushes and cattle feed. Heather rope was found in the Neolithic settlement of Skara Brae in Orkney which dates back some 5,000 years. People lived simple lives and they lived in harmony with heather.

Bonnie blooming heather, carpeting the hillside and stretching as far as the eye can see, has been celebrated in song and verse. It is a sight to gladden the heart of the tourist and native Scot alike, as essential a part of the Scottish image as the deer and the golden eagle. However, the carpet is now getting a bit ragged round the edges – worn so thin in some places that it has disappeared altogether.

The heather moorland of the world is now virtually confined to Britain and Ireland, occupying the area between enclosed farms and the treeline. Although heather moorland still covers around 38 per cent of Scotland's landscape, almost

25 per cent of the cover has been lost since the Second World War. The problem in Scotland is not so much the trampling feet of tourists and hillwalkers but overgrazing, blanket afforestation, together with too rigorous burning, bracken spread and insect infestation. Disappearance of heather leaves bare ground on which it can never regenerate. Along fence lines the heather can be vigorous on one side and absent on the other because of different land management techniques. Heather has been noted retreating up the hillsides in the glacial valleys of Scotland.

Some wonder if the loss of heather is such a big deal. From every standpoint – heritage, environment, conservation – the answer has to be a resounding yes. It's an integral part of the environment for Highlanders and Lowlanders alike and with the loss of patches of heather whole ecosystems vanish. It's said that forty bird species depend on it, including the red grouse. If people would throw away their j-pods and commune with nature once again catastrophes such as the vanishing heather moors can still be avoided.

Letitia Marrow
Smokey Bottom, Ilfracombe, Devon

Insular Attitudes

I have followed the recent exchange about the number of islands in Loch Lomond with great interest. It seems there is just as much confusion over the number of Scottish islands: there seems to be somewhere between 400 and 700 depending on which source one consults. Which Scottish island is officially the nation's smallest and how small can an island be and still qualify for that description?

Isla St Bonita
8 Hebridean Circle, East Kilbride, Lanarkshire

Small islands are extraordinary places, with their rugged salt spray coasts shaped by the forces of time and tide. Each island has its own history, heritage and sense of place. But Miss Bonita is correct to question the definition of an island. On the surface, if you'll pardon the pun, it seems quite a straightforward business. An island is a piece of land surrounded by water. But is it really that easy? An island, I would argue, is much more than that. For example, going by the strict geographical definition we would have to include places such as Australia and Antarctica.

But surely these are also continents, vast areas with a tremendous variation in climate and topography, making it very difficult to get a sense of place. So, in searching for the definition of an island, if there's a sandbank, or a bridge, or a tunnel or a causeway, does that disqualify our candidate as an island? There is an argument for just that, and it will occur to your readers that this would nowadays disqualify what is arguably Scotland's most famous island – Skye. Not to mention the United Kingdom itself.

Brave souls in Scotland have tried over the centuries to come up with a definition of an island. There is even, perhaps inevitably, an official one. In the 1861 census the editors defined an island as a piece of land surrounded by water which has sufficient vegetation to support a couple of sheep for a year – and almost as an afterthought they added: 'or is inhabited by man'.

In the past few years a gent named Hamish Haswell-Smith brought out a wonderful gazetteer of Scotland's islands. For our purposes his definition of an island is interesting. He asserts that if you can wade across to a piece of land at low tide then it can't qualify as an island. This would mean that our sandbanks, causeways, etc. did indeed remove island status.

All things being equal I think we might be as well to stick to the 1861 census and work by the Two Sheep Principle.

John Stornoway
14 Appalachian Walkway, Oban

Whenever this debate about what constitutes an island arises, I can't look past a book published in the 1930s called *Orkney – the Magnetic North* in which the author, Gunn, comes up with the interesting proposition that an island must feel like an island. You must feel as if you can easily walk – or sail – around the isle and the sea must be visible from most parts of the island.

This clearly gets controversial because it disqualifies our super-islands such as Greenland, Sri Lanka, Iceland, Australia – and, of course, Great Britain. We fall on two counts, in fact, not only are we too big, but we are joined to France by a tunnel. At the other end of the scale, surely countless small, rocky tidal outcrops and skerries must be scored off the list of real islands. They are more part of the sea than the land. Somewhere on the borderline between tidal skerry and island will lie Miss Bonita's smallest Scottish island. Identifying it, well that's another matter altogether.

Pink Dochart
The Narrows, Rhu, West Dunbartonshire

Has anyone considered the possibility that an island is only an island if there is someone there to look at it? Deserted islands may be atmospheric but to me they are infinitely sad places. They represent a failure, for whatever reason, to sustain a viable community. The hearths are cold, the gardens neglected, the fields unattended. They may be islands in the strict geographical definition but they lack the vital ingredient to breathe life into them – people!

Professor Al B. Jenzian
Dept of Celtic Mysteries,
University of the Montana Highlands, Butte, USA

C'mon, Get Aff!

What and where is Auchenshuggle? A student in this department is suggesting that it is simply another Brigadoon.

Regius Professor Essex Hain
Department of Philology and Strange Words, Caledonian University, Augusta, Georgia, USA

I can't imagine where you stumbled across this place name, Professor, but Auchenshuggle is an almost legendary terminus, a bit like Camelot with a timetable, on the now defunct Glasgow tramcar network. Many a mantelpiece in Glasgow is decorated with a bent penny from the last run of the tram – between Auchenshuggle and Dalmuir West – before the system shut down in 1962. Kids placed the coins in the tracks and the tram ran over the pennies, crushing them into memorable keepsakes.

Auchenshuggle lies south of Tollcross, four miles southeast of the city centre. The site of a small settlement in the nineteenth century, this oddly named location came to prominence in 1922 as the eastern terminus of the Number 9 tram, which ran from Dalmuir (West Dunbartonshire), via Yoker, Scotstoun and Partick through the city centre to Auchenshuggle until 1962. The curious began to take this tram solely to visit what became, in the first half of the twentieth century, an internationally famous Scottish place name.

Adam Thom
14 Depot Drive, Blairgowrie

I've been intrigued to hear all the fascinating information about Auchenshuggle but I have, reluctantly, to throw a spanner into the wheels. When I was a boy in the 1950s I travelled occasionally on the Number 9 Auchenshuggle to Dalmuir West to visit an elderly aunt. Naturally, being an inquisitive young chap I inquired about the name Auchenshuggle. Now, my dad had been a driver on the trams before switching professions and moving into the used car business. I recall quite clearly him telling me that the name had been made up by an enterprising member of the Corporation transport staff in order to attract visitors to make tram journeys.

If this is the case then that was certainly a success. Many passengers admitted to making the journey out along London Road in the tram car simply to be able to say they had visited Auchenshuggle, a quintessentially Scottish community – but as legendary, elusive and, indeed, as unreal as Brigadoon.

Pastor William Burke
4th Day Protectionists, Bonar Bridge, Ross and Cromarty

As a matter of interest, the famous tram Number 9 was replaced by the Number 64 bus which still makes the journey every half-hour to Auchenshuggle. With a slightly different spelling, Auchenshoogle became the fictional home town of Oor Wullie, the Scots comic book hero. The trams on the Auchenshuggle run were garaged at Partick.

Sammy McInespie
Siltart Cove, Dorset

It was with disbelief that I read Pastor Burke's letter revisiting that old myth about the name Auchenshuggle having been coined by an imaginative member of Glasgow Corporation Transport. Auchenshuggle, I can testify, having grown up there, is as real as your magazine and your legion of correspondents from all over the world.

Auchenshuggle is to be found in London Road at the foot of Braidfauld Road and the name is thought to derive from the Gaelic for 'fields of corn'. It isn't so long ago that the Tollcross area was indeed on the outskirts of the city on fertile, crop-growing land. In the nineteenth century it was a self-contained little community including a number of large, smart houses and the manse of St Margaret's, Tollcross.

The myth of the bureaucratic naming probably came about because, although the area was known universally as Auchenshuggle by the people who lived there, no signs confirming this were to be found in the streets. It is unfortunate that the place became the butt of music hall jokes because in reality it was a district of fine open countryside and lovely people and I can remember as clearly as if it was yesterday the sound of the 'six o'clock' bell which told the field workers that it was time to knock off for the night.

Verity Meadows
The Thatched Cottage, Scrag End, Gloucestershire

Shakin' All Over

My auntie in Arbroath has a china teapot which was damaged during an earthquake at Comrie sometime in the 1800s. Surely earthquakes are very rare in Scotland?

Sharon 'Shakin' Stevens
Jordanhill, Glasgow

There is a popular misconception that Britain is not an important focus of earthquake activity. In fact, the most seismic parts of Britain are to be found in Scotland. The Great Glen is a splendid example of a fault line and lying on its track, Inverness was a victim of significant earthquakes in 1769, 1816, 1888 and 1901.

The small Perthshire village of Comrie, mentioned by Sharon Stevens, became the earthquake capital of Europe in the nineteenth century after it experienced a remarkable 7,000 tremors – three of them significant – during a seven-year period up to 1846. Little wonder it still carries the nickname of 'The Shaky Toun'. As a result of this remarkable sequence of events the first earthquake observatory was established in the community, which in turn gave rise to the science of seismology.

Recent surveys have indicated fault lines in rocks deep below Britain and the seas which surround us. A quake on a significant scale is possible in the United Kingdom at any time.

Dr Sam Andreas
Lamlash, Isle of Arran

Scotland, despite what Miss Stevens seems to believe, is a very important centre of earthquake activity. For connoisseurs of exquisite coincidences can I cite the powerful earth tremor of 1984 which shook several places in the West of Scotland including Glasgow. It is a fact that at the precise moment the tremor struck BBC Radio 2 was playing The Beach Boys' 'Good Vibrations'.

Alabama Lambert
Venice Beach, Stenhousemuir, Stirlingshire

Sharon Stevens' teapot was lucky to survive according to some of the stories which have emerged from Comrie over the years. When the intense period of earthquake activity began in the village in 1839 a correspondent sent detailed reports to the *Inverness Courier*, extracts from which indicate why Comrie subsequently became such an important centre for the study of earth movements. These reports speak of unusual effects such as the wind dropping immediately before the tremors. On Saturday, 12 October that year, ten shocks in all were felt at Comrie. The correspondent indicates that during the first, third and ninth of these shocks, slates fell from roofs, stones dislodged from walls and crockery moved around (presumably including the Stevens family's china teapot).

Events of 23 October took a much more serious turn after an 'indescribably dreadful shock' about 10.30 p.m. It resembled the 'noise of many thunders' (obviously there was a Cherokee living in the village) and was followed by torrential rain, which caused the River Earn to burst its banks. The whole population took shelter in the Secession Church, expecting at any moment to be swept away or dropped into the pit of despond.

Dr Stanley Bullock
The Rectory, Stiffkey-on-Sea, Sussex

I've read that around 300 earthquakes are recorded every year north of the Border. Like disease and meteorological events, in centuries past, earthquakes were apparently seen as evidence of God's wrath. Earthquakes in Scotland have, in the twentieth century, offered endless and unexpected opportunities for fun, especially when the British Geological Survey distribute inane questionnaires in an effort to establish the exact nature of a particular tremor. The possibilities can be seen in questions such as: 'Did any hanging objects swing?' or 'Did anything else rattle?' As for the question 'Were you sitting, standing, lying down, sleeping, active, listening to TV or radio?' – this could open up more than just a can of worms. In the Lothians some twentieth-century tremors were attributed to mining activity. Clearly since the destruction of the British coal industry these reports are considerably fewer.

Sun Dim Yon Macrae
The Star of Bengal Indian Restaurant,
Carstairs, Lanarkshire

So we get earthquakes in Scotland which damage teapots? Big deal. Perhaps we should get things into perspective. Hundreds of thousands have died in earthquakes in recent years, notably in China in 1976, and the mother of all earthquakes was surely that of 1201 when one million people are thought to have died in the Middle East. The Lisbon earthquake of 1775 killed up to 100,000 people and temporarily raised the water level in Loch Lomond.

Thomas Richter
Villa Verde, Skaill, Orkney

Messrs Stiffkey and Co. are painting only a partial picture of the effects of earthquakes on Scotland. For some reason Comrie seems to be regularly resurrected to serve as a classic Caledonian example of seismic activity. What about Fife? During the Great Fife Earthquake of AD 811 – before Kenneth McAlpin got round to pulling the Picts and Scots together to form our nation – the East Neuk of Fife, and in particular the St Andrews area, was said to have been devastated by an earthquake which killed 1,400 people and severely damaged almost every building in the region. Further shocks in this general area were reported in 1801, 1816, 1841, 1890 and 1979. On the west coast, Arran was shaken in March 1999 by Scotland's biggest earthquake in seventy years. The event took place on the seabed three miles south of the island. It was reported that beds were given a 'good shaking' around midnight. Scotland's largest earthquake, 5.2 on the scale, took place in 1880 and was centred near Loch Awe.

Just to emphasise that there are plenty of 'Shaky Touns' in Scotland, may I point out that the Kessock Bridge lying on the Great Glen fault line was fitted with 'shock absorbers' to soak up any seismic activity.

C. Latter
Glen Tilt, Perthshire

Long-Sighted and How!

What is the greatest distance claimed to have been seen with the naked eye in Scotland?

Alec Glancy
Bella Vista, Sighthill, Edinburgh

As someone who is short-sighted, living in a permanent impressionist haze, the idea of seeing vast distances across the Scottish landscape is a weird concept. Seeing family members on the other side of the street is enough of a challenge. But instances of stunning long-distance sightings are actually quite plentiful. In World War II soldiers from the Eighth Army stationed in the Campinile, Italy, claimed to have seen Mont Blanc, 250 miles away from their artillery observation post, and an Oxford man saw Mount McKinley in Alaska from 200 miles away.

One of the most impressive Scottish claims is the 150-mile sighting in 1969 of the hills of Donegal by a group of climbers on Beinn Sguliaird in Lorne, Argyll. This becomes all the more impressive when you learn that an equivalent distance would be Aberdeen to Carlisle.

Benjamin More
The Bothy, Hill o' Beath, Fife

The mechanics of long-distance sightings are interesting. Mountains and a dust-free airstream from the north have definitely placed Scotland in the front line of such events. Glimpses of locations beyond the horizon are possible because of a phenomenon known as the curvature of light rays. Layers of air at different temperatures cause an image of the hills to be lifted above the horizon by light refraction.

Claire Vijon
Centre for Talking About Folk with Wonderful Sight,
Eyemouth, Berwickshire

In Orkney's North Isles the story is told of how, for several hours one morning in the 1940s, the image of the coastline of Norway around the city of Bergen appeared away to the east. It was identified by someone on the island of Sanday who had visited that coast. This is a remarkable 270–300 miles away from the beaches of Orkney.

Mavis Grind
The Midden, Stormay, Orkney

Vicky's Pit Stops?

Scotland seems to be studded with stone rock piles which I am told
are called cairns. Is it true, as our tour bus driver Darren indicated,
that these were all erected at locations where Queen Victoria stopped
to have a picnic or to admire the view?

Milan Soderoff
Via Carmina del Piero, Terni, Umbria, Italy

You must be very careful, Signor Soderoff, about taking
history from the mouth of a bus driver at face value. Scotland's
history is dark, dangerous and confusing enough without
swallowing the gospel according to someone from Surbiton
or Basingstoke whose knowledge of Scottish history is based
on the fact that he has seen *Braveheart* twice.

Cairns are indeed very numerous, particularly in the
Highlands, and their purposes are many. It has been a Gaelic
custom for the past 1,500 years to raise a cairn of loose stones
to commemorate a person or an event – a death in the snow, a
drowning, a battle or a skirmish – which by personal or general
consensus should not be forgotten. Sadly, many of the stories
explaining the siting of such cairns have been lost forever as
the Highlands were depopulated. These informal cairns, of
course, differ from the huge, formal cemented versions with
memorial plaques which are also widely found.

The unofficial commemorative cairns are very similar
indeed to those which top so many of our mountains and
date from the days of the Ordnance Survey. Many of these
were piled up by engineers in order to give themselves
sighting points. Other mountain-top cairns have accumulated
over the centuries as visitors to the summits felt they had to
mark their achievement by adding a stone to the heap.

Cairns found along the shore often identify the spot where a victim of drowning had been washed ashore. Resting cairns or *suidhe* in Gaelic are also found along remote roads. These were built along the routes taken by funeral parties to the graveyard; often the trek for those bearing the coffin could be ten or twenty miles.

Oh yes, just a few cairns, Signor Soderoff, were indeed built to mark Victoria's pit stops, particularly in the north-east of Scotland.

Paul Fraser
Custodian, Cairns are Fun, Portsoy, Banffshire

There is considerable nonsense talked about the presence of cairns throughout the Scottish landscape. These are not commemorative piles, as is often suggested, but rather, as has always been quite clear to me, these were the very first tactical deterrent. When your neighbours, or the Romans, or the Picts noised you up and threatened to torch your clachan, you simply retreated up the hill and waiting at the top was a neatly stacked pile of ammunition which you could hurl at your enemy as he peched wearily up the hillside.

Ranald Burgoyne-Tosh (Lt Col. Rtd)
West Perthshire Yeomanry, Battlefield House, Kenmore

7

Pride and prejudice

⊛ Granite Hearts?

Are folk in Aberdeen really the dourest of the dour and the meanest of the mean as they are often portrayed?

Richard Cheery
Sunnybraes, Pasadena, California, USA

We should all be greatly indebted to Richard Cheery for giving us the opportunity to clear up this latest anti-Aberdonian myth. It's bad enough that Aberdonians have been mistakenly labelled for so many years as being tight-fisted – now we are being accused of sullenness, a totally unwarranted and scurrilous accusation.

The suggestion that we are mean has, in fact, been thoroughly discredited in recent times. So I will not revisit that nonsensical suggestion. Suffice to say that charity giving in Aberdeen compares very favourably with any other large city in the UK.

Now, it seems we must defend ourselves against accusations of being gloomy, cheerless and staid. This is just as easily done.

Scotland has a maritime climate, which, in essence, means lots of rain. Go anywhere through our great nation and you will find that when grey skies and rain descend the effect is similar. People hurry to get inside to the warmth beside a cheery fire and have little time for passing pleasantries. But there is an additional problem in Aberdeen. Not only do the people appear grey under eight-eighths cloud cover, our buildings are constructed from grey granite. The people and their backdrop mysteriously fuse in the rainy, dark months into a uniformly grey landscape. The picture could indeed be interpreted as a city living under a mournful blanket.

However, this does not in any sense mean that their hearts are not singing, although it may look that way to an outsider. They are simply awaiting a reawakening. And the key to this renaissance is, of course, the sun. The winter visitor must return to Aberdeen in the beautiful, sharp, crystal-clear days of spring when the sunshine sparkles on the granite and the city – and its people come splendidly alive. No dourness can be traced in this emerging. See the smiles in Union Street, the laughter in Duthie Park, the cheerful conversations in King Street, the chirpiness of brilliant young people on the campuses of the two city universities and around the schools.

You will struggle to find across the length and breadth of Scotland a city that is more comfortably and happily at home with itself than Aberdeen.

Constance Baggladie
Third bench down from the Wallace Monument, Union Terrace, Aberdeen

It was nice to hear from Constance again after her spell in Cornhill. However, as usual, she has got the wrong end of the stick completely. We do have a particular problem here in the north and the long faces are not restricted to folk trailing down King Street after the latest comedy of errors at Pittodrie.

A surprisingly large number of people in the north-east of Scotland, some say up to 5 per cent of the population, suffer seriously from seasonal affective disorder (SAD), which, rather worryingly, is a higher percentage than the people of Scandinavia. Apparently as many as 20 per cent of people in the north-east display some symptoms of the problem.

SAD, attributed to the suffocating darkness of our long winter nights, usually manifests itself in anxiety attacks, depression, difficulty getting up in the morning, lack of motivation, cravings for carbohydrates, weight gain, lethargy and tiredness.

Little wonder then that in the depths of winter there are long faces, surly expressions, and angry exchanges in the shops and bus queues, on the factory floor and in the pubs.

People, deprived of the warmth of the sun, are narked and stressed and the city can indeed seem dour and unwelcoming as a result.

Having outlined the problem I really should offer some sort of solution. Light deprivation is clearly at the root of the problem. We simply can't wait for the sun to start sparkling on the granite. The simplest answer is to make use of what winter sunlight there is to wash away the miseries – get out into what little daylight there is. Constance is correct. Gloom is not the natural state of the Aberdonian but in this, the most northerly city in Britain (lying further north than Moscow, believe it or not), we have a special problem.

To bring the smiles back on the Aberdonian faces we might consider opening sunlight cafes where folk could soak up summertime daylight from specially made light boxes which have already brought relief from the blues for so many.

Sol Brightmore
Daybreak, Ellon, Aberdeenshire

A Scottish Affair

What precisely is Scotophobia? It sounds as if it should be a terror of all things Scots and of Scotland – but I'm told that this is not so.

Ina Fleming
The Heilan' Hame, Beach Parade, Killin, Perthshire

Scotophobia is not, as you might expect, an irrational fear of hairy-arsed Scots singing 'Flower of Scotland' or belting out a reel on the bagpipes. The complaint describes a dread of darkness, deriving from the Greek word skotos (darkness).

However, a terror of all things Caledonian is not an uncommon experience, particularly for people living south of the Border. More accurately it might be described as a loathing or, even more disappointingly, a total indifference to all things Scottish. For every English settler who has made Scotland his or her home over the past thirty years there must be 100 other stay-at-homes who would never consider visiting Scotland voluntarily and still firmly believe it is nothing more than a forlorn northern English county, the home of rebellious hill folk.

This suspicion of Scotland and the Scots stems, of course, from the Jacobite Uprising of 1745 which brought the Highland army to within sniffing distance of London and gave the good citizens of the English capital a serious fright. But generally, over a period of 2,000 years the Scots have been portrayed as a barbarian crew.

Rehabilitation of the Scots began almost immediately after Culloden, when the wild clans were finally seen to be tamed, and it was further helped along by Queen Victoria and Sir Walter Scott but the centuries of indoctrination have had their effect. It is reckoned from a survey by the Scottish tourist industry that almost half the people living in England have never crossed the Border even for a weekend break and have absolutely no desire to venture into the badlands.

Alec Moraine
Terminal 1, Leith Docks, by Edinburgh

Scotophobia is a fear of darkness but I would suggest that it might just as easily describe an acute anxiety over the way in which, ever since the Union, the Scots have beaten a path to London where they seem determined to take control of everything that matters in English society from the government to the management of football teams.

Is it any wonder that true Englishmen have a fear of the Scots and their gnawing ambition? The Union of 1707 has brought England nothing but trouble and if it ends next year it will be two centuries too late. We subsidise the Scots, propping them up with countless billions, and not a word of thanks do we hear from north of the Border, from the land which playwright Jonathan Miller called the People's Democratic Socialist Republic of Caledonia.

It might be a great idea to simply let them get on with running their own country. They would soon find out just how much they needed the much-reviled English. Yes, set Scotland adrift by all means. There would be an immediate and stunning reduction in tax here in England, and Westminster would immediately be rid of its most tedious windbags.

Kurt Anzer
Longbottom Priory, Friendship Row,
Canterbury, Kent

◉ Fol de Rol

Do trolls exist or are they just peerie, angry Shetlanders?

Persephone Silk-Like (Miss)
Utter Lane, Bottingley, Hants.

The kingdom of the fairy folk, an entrance to which certainly lies beneath a hill near you, is vast and many tribes are contained therein: hobgoblins, elves, faeries, imps – and trolls. These little people – known more often in Shetland and Orkney as trows or trowie folk – are mentioned in the folklore so frequently you have to think that these are not just the wild imaginings of some unstable soul or the rantings of an Unst man who has partaken over-freely of the home brew.

The fact that they tend now to be treated as a merely a couthy myth, I believe, is simply because in this technological, self-satisfied society folk do not have the capacity to separate themselves from the hard grind of day-to-day life and see what a wonderful, surprising place the world really is and to perceive what is actually going on around them.

It's thought that the first trowies came from Norway in the holds of the longships, pretending to be bags o' grain. They found the mounds and monuments of the Neolithic folk gave them a perfect home. If the trolls do not exist then it is very difficult to explain away the place names of Shetland and Orkney which seem to signal their presence – Inner Trolla, Trolligart, Trolladale, to name just three of dozens of such names.

The record of these shadowy people is extensive and makes it possible to build up a pretty comprehensive composite picture of the troll. Generally they are a good deal smaller and uglier than the average man, fond of music, mischievous and they like to dress in grey. Their children were often weak and sickly and the troll might attempt to switch them for a human child. One of their nastiest habits was leaving stocks or replicas of the person they were kidnapping. They were fond of fire, stealing into the houses when their own fire went out, and fleeing with a supply of sparks which most Shetlanders in the past must have seen scuttling across the floor from hearth to front door.

The trowie love of music, particularly fiddle music, is interesting and is reflected in the human cultural scene in Shetland and Orkney to this day, both island groups having their own flourishing folk festivals. Keep your eyes open at the free sessions – the ugly wee man on the fiddle may be from under the hill!

Tasker Firth
Aboon the Bog, Walls, Shetland

There can be little doubt that trolls or trowies exist or, at least, did exist in some form in the past. However, there is always a strong mystical element in the story of the hill folk. You see, the trowies were not visible to everyone. There is a powerful suggestion that they would never appear to non-believers. We live in a cynical, pragmatic world which has lost touch with the feel of the grass and the wind whispering in your ear – non-believers abound. It is distinctly possible that we are walking past trowies in the street. Believing is seeing.

We tend to think of the trolls as mythical creatures from the ancient past, their struggles with mankind probably representing, the sociologists and anthropologists tell us, the strains and stresses between the old Roman faith and the new Reformed religion. Fine that as an explanation, as far as it goes.

However, what about the story from World War II collected by the folklorist Ernest Marwick about a serviceman who was alone on the cliffs at Torness on Hoy on a day of fierce winds when he found himself in the midst of a group of about a dozen tiny, mean-looking 'wild men' who danced around him? For two or three minutes they cavorted about before appearing to throw themselves over the cliff.

So next time some wee bloke pushes past you in the supermarket queue in Lerwick or Kirkwall, just be cautious in case, when you noise him up, he tries to steal you away tae Elfhame.

Rod Pagett
Braes of Quindeck, Sanday, Orkney

The Eye of the Beholder

Scotland has four world heritage sites – St Kilda, Orkney, Edinburgh and New Lanark – others such as the Forth Rail Bridge, the Cairngorms, the Caithness Flow country and the Antonine Wall wait in the wings. Is this not a rather unimaginative selection?

Margaret Park (Ms)
Rowardennan, Loch Lomondside

We must never overlook the fact that already having four world heritage sites is a stupendous achievement for a nation the size of Scotland. However, I do agree that the whole idea should be widened to include locations which might not immediately or obviously spring to mind. Perhaps I can set the ball rolling. As a commercial driver, I would like to nominate an inconspicuous lay-by on the A9 about five miles south of Helmsdale. Driving north, I always aim for twenty minutes' shut-eye there in the wee sma' hours before pressing on to Wick or Thurso. At this sanctuary I have had some of the sweetest sleep I can remember.

Dick Restalrig
Premium Meat Pies, St Fillings Street, Elgin

Excuse me, but Mr Restalrig seems to have completely lost the plot. The idea is to have sites of beauty, interest and significance to the nation, not some God-forsaken spot where he has a kip. No, we must think big. I would like to nominate the Ikea superstore in Glasgow which has brought the people of the West of Scotland together in a way that politicians, preachers or football teams have failed to do. And, honestly, in the light of evening the building itself can look impressive – a sort of golden temple to twenty-first-century commercialism. Seeing it on such evenings almost brings a tear to the eye – or perhaps that's just the exhaust fumes in the car park.

Pieter ver Plank
Sunnyside Cottage, Penpont, Dumfriesshire

These final two letters close this long-running correspondence. We are surprised to find that in our straw poll of responses, Nardini's ice-cream parlour in Largs edged out the Forth Rail Bridge as our readers' choice for the next World Heritage Site — Ed.

Sacrilege!

An English acquaintance says that the haggis as a dish was introduced to Scotland by the French. Can this possibly be true?

Herbert Currie
The Cattle Shed, Friockheim, Angus

Once again a false rumour designed to undermine Scottish self-confidence is being peddled. The Great Chieftain o' the

Puddin' Race – our national dish, brought out triumphantly at Hogmanay, St Andrew's Night and Burns Night, seems to be quintessentially Scottish; you might even say that the reek o' the haggis o'er the glens is what made Scotland. But are its origins thoroughly Scottish or is it all down to Robbie Burns putting it on the culinary and literary map some 200 years ago?

It is known that the Greeks had a form of haggis, similar to our own much-loved sheep's paunch. The Romans, who specialised in bizarre food items including deep-fried dormouse and curried larks' tongues, reputedly carried haggis all round Europe in their kit bags. Immortalised by Aristophanes in *The Clouds*, the remarkable description of an exploding haggis and a startled chef was recounted by Scottish food writer F. Marian McNeill (1885–1973):

> Why, now the murder's out!
> So was I served with a stuffed paunch I broiled,
> On Jove's day last, just such a scurvy trick;
> Because, forsooth, not dreaming of your thunder,
> I never thought to give the rascal vent,
> Bounce, goes the bag, and covers me all over,
> With its rich contents.

The possible origins of the word are interesting and any lingering Scottish jingoism in relation to the haggis is quickly dispelled when the etymology is put under the microscope. One plausible explanation which suggests a French connection is that haggis is a corruption of the word *hachis* or minced meat. Another school of thought traces it to the medieval Scandinavian word *hag* which meant to hack or chop. In Sweden *pölsa* is almost identical to haggis.

Whatever, it was in Scotland that the haggis found its

spiritual home. Venison and beef haggis were made but it is the mutton version with which most Scots are familiar. A dish that started off as the frugal fare of the agricultural classes probably in the early Middle Ages was, by the early nineteenth century, being enjoyed at posh dinner tables. Once again we have an aspect of Scottish culture, like the kilt and bagpipes, which it would be well-nigh impossible to prove as our invention, but there is absolutely no doubt that the haggis evolved in Scotland. The Great Chieftain is as Scottish as Jimmy Krankie.

Elvin Foot
Minutes Secretary, Burns Club of the Knox Coast,
Antarctica

Everyone seems determined to prove that some Roman centurion or Greek transvestite invented Scotland's national dish. Of course, it was your national bard Robert Burns who identified the haggis with the concept of Scottish nationhood, brotherhood and sisterhood and brought the idea of haggis eating to a wider audience. Within a few years of his classic poem being published the nobility were devouring haggis enthusiastically. However, the Great Chieftain had been around in Scotland for a thousand years before that.

Elvin Foot mentioned Dr Marian McNeill – she also described the haggis as a 'super-sausage' and who is going to disagree with that? In fact, she identified four reasons why the haggis in its present form found a natural environment in Scotland: first of all, Scots' thrift demanded much be made of very little; the imaginative use of pinmeal in the dish reflected Caledonian enterprise; haggis became classless, reflecting the egalitarian nature of Scottish society; and, fourthly, the use of a paunch pleased the nation's fondness for 'romantic barbarism'.

Dr McNeill also pondered why the sausage should have become a civilised dish while the haggis remained a barbarian dish everywhere outside Scotland (except in the Scots diaspora, of course). It remains an interesting question but I suspect it results from efforts to eradicate or stigmatise Highland culture after the Jacobite Uprising of 1745.

Murdo Lichterweld
Association of Horse Butchers, Bruges, Belgium

It is not a pretty sight – the Scots jumping to the defence of the indefensible. If it wasn't for the fact that folk north of the Border are such notable whingers, the government would have banned the haggis long ago. It can scarcely be described as a food – more a repository for the leftovers of the slaughtering process.

There is no doubt in my mind that the paranoid defensive posture taken by Scots over a thousand issues, including the origins of haggis, results from criticism of the Scots by folk like Samuel Johnson who wisecracked that oats, normally fed to horses in England, is the staple for Scots.

Rev. Roger Pedant
Bury St Edmunds, Suffolk

The Answer, My Friend

There seems to be a great deal of anxiety about the renewable energy programme, in particular the development of wind power and how such a programme might destroy Scotland's scenic beauty. Will a new Caledonian forest of wind generators really be such an eyesore?

Adrian Storm
The Avenue, Padstow, Cornwall

I think wind generators are a hideous blot on the beautiful mountains of Scotland and those already constructed should be dismantled. They are symbols of a society which has lost sight of the value of unspoiled landscape, of the sacred nature of place.

Planners, councillors, engineers and developers who are pushing the idea that renewable energy is the solution to all our problems should hang their heads with shame. Let the hills of Scotland stay as they always have been – starkly beautiful and devoid of the unnecessary monstrosities of the modern age.

Once again I repeat my call that we should harness the methane gas produced by the nation's vast herds of cows to provide basic essential power.

Letitia Marrow (Ms)
Smokey Bottom, Ilfracombe

So much hot air has been produced on the topic of wind generators in the style of Ms Marrow that it is surprising that we are even having the opportunity to contemplate their use in Scotland at all. Let's look for a moment at the landscape which people consider will be ruined by their arrival and, more specifically, let's briefly examine one development that has already taken place.

That is on the edge of the Caithness flow country between Thurso and Latheron where a group of generators are spinning away merrily in the empty land. Anyone who claims that this development has taken away from the amenity of the area is either blind or living in a parallel universe. Wind generators are a vital component in the world's energy programme for the rest of this century. More importantly they are wondrous to behold.

These turbines are simply magnificent – tall, statuesque, graceful and giving the passing motorist a sense of the awesome power of how the natural elements dominate in this part of the world, the huge blades sweeping round and round in a truly hypnotic manner. That is, in fact, probably the only negative aspect of the development I can think of: it might be a distraction, a driving hazard. They have transformed what was a bleak and generally featureless landscape where the most exciting thing between Thurso and Latheron was a peat extraction facility. Now, you need to be pretty desperate to get excited over peat.

Much of what British culture has received from America over the past half-century has been of questionable value but the realisation that these wind generators are things of beauty which can transform a drab, uninteresting landscape into a surreal and magical place has been one of the most positive messages to come out of America.

In the same way that the flatlands of Belgium have been made much more distinctive and interesting by the addition of groves of wind generators, so the wild, bare places of Scotland will be revitalised by this new Caledonian forest. Scotland must not be left behind in this exciting new technology.

Fulton Catchett
Wind for the People, Hilltop, Braemar

I am happy that the wild places of Scotland should be used to develop wind power. Apart from hunting they are really of no great value and strangely empty of people. My only real concern is that these huge turbines may frighten grouse and make stalking difficult. As long as these concerns are addressed and the wind generators cannot be seen from

Calton Hill, I believe that we as a nation should applaud their introduction.

Symphonia Dufftown
Morningside, Edinburgh

My Delight

The history of the kilt and the tartans – components of Scotland's 'national dress' – is very confusing. For example, I've heard it suggested that the kilt was the invention of an Englishman. And where exactly do trews fit into the picture?

Keith Fraser
Tartan House, Plaid Road, Grangemouth

The history of the kilt is indeed about as dark and convoluted as the story of Scotland itself. I believe that the 'belted plaid' and its later adaptations – the philabeg or short kilt – were indeed the invention of an English Quaker contractor who worked on the construction of a network of roads in the Highlands after the Jacobite Uprising of 1715. However, another English contractor employed at Strontian in Argyll also gets the credit for this sartorial breakthrough.

Of course, the long plaid was worn by Highlanders for centuries, perhaps millennia, before this likely English interference took place. It was used as a wrap-around blanket for sleeping, as well as daytime wear, and getting it on properly seems to have been an art in itself.

Not only is the short kilt probably the product of English interference, the word kilt itself may well be English. Some sources say it derives from 'quilt' because of the pleated effect in the garment and the fact that it was also used as a sleeping garment.

Another possibility is that it may have a Norse root – 'to kilt' in Middle English means to hitch or tuck up a skirt.

It is assumed that in the 1700s the English overseers felt that the plaid hampered the manual work required of the local labour and suggested belting up as a means of tidying up their act. However, if anyone should take responsibility for the kilt becoming our national dress it must surely be Sir Walter Scott, who organised a party for the visit of George IV in 1822. Clan chiefs turned out in force and the portly monarch even got himself kitted out in a mini-kilt and pink tights. That should have been enough to consign the kilt to oblivion. The fact that it instead raised it to sartorial pre-eminence just goes to show what a contrary lot the Scots are.

As to the origin of trews and their place in the story of the kilt, I fear I cannot assist, but I have read that officers in the Jacobite army on the march south to Derby during the '45 wore a tartan doublet, trews and a plaid. That the army as a whole was dressed in the short kilt is confirmed by a statement from Bonnie Prince Charlie's aide-de-camp, Lord George Murray, who speaks of being 'on this day in my philabeg, that is to say without britches . . . nothing encouraged the men more than seeing their officers dressed like themselves.'

I think that Scots should just be happy that they have such a distinctive national garb. Does it really matter who invented or restyled it in the dim and distant past? Rejoice at the splendour of the kilt, wear it with pride, you Scots.

Joy Bliss
Institute for Being Really Cheerful,
1 Commando Terrace, Aldershot

Trews were never a peculiarly Scottish form of dress although once again this looks like an instance where the Scots appear to have made them their own. Celtic tribes in the centuries before Christ wore tight-fitting, brightly coloured trousers and the trouserless Romans regarded the wearing of trews as yet another sign of barbarian culture. The word trews comes from the Irish Gaelic *truis*, a garment which appears in the eighth-century *Book of Kells* which, although housed in Ireland, is thought to have been created at the Columban monastery on Iona.

Tartan trews in the modern setting are first recorded in the first half of the sixteenth century, worn as protection against the cold both by gentry and ordinary clansfolk. By the early 1700s the nobility, and in particular military commanders, had adopted the style as their own. Trews looked best on weel-proportioned men – they did not flatter the flabby. During the years between 1746 and 1782, when the kilt was banned, plain-coloured trews continued to be worn in the north. By the nineteenth century, trews were worn only on ceremonial occasions by officers of the Highland regiments, the neatly pressed trouser having made its mark.

Cormac McButter
Trews Protection League, Good Grief, Iowa, USA

Shared Roots

Is it true that Glasgow Green played an important part in the formation of both Celtic and Rangers football clubs?

Bob B. Shaftow
Fisherman's Wharf, Campbeltown, Argyll

Once again we find football creeping insidiously into every aspect of life in Scotland. Do people not realise that the wide acres of Glasgow Green have a fascinating history apart altogether from its connection with the Old Firm? This history has included regular courtroom battles to prevent drastic changes in use of this precious space in the heart of the city. Most recently there was a successful campaign to halt a plan to drive an elevated or tunnelled motorway across the Green.

To get Mr Shaftow's question out of the way before attending to meatier matters, we should confirm that, in 1872, Rangers FC (not Glasgow Rangers as everyone seems to want to call them) was constituted on the Green, the focus for football in the city since the Middle Ages, and, five years later, at St Mary's Church Hall, Calton, on the fringes of the Green, Celtic FC was formed.

Glasgow Green has provided a fascinating barometer of Glasgow's social and cultural development since it was first gifted to the people of the district as common grazing by the Church in 1450. For centuries the open spaces beside the Clyde performed this valuable community role. The Green reappears in the history books in 1745 when the Jacobite army of Bonnie Prince Charlie camped at a site known as Flesher's Haugh en route to Derby during the Uprising. Glasgow was pro-government and had no love for the dashing Prince, especially when, during his stay, he threatened to put the city to the torch. Having a change of heart, he settled for a few civic dignitaries as hostages.

Over the years the Green has performed a wide variety of functions. It was here, according to tradition, that James Watt happened on the idea of a steam condenser while out for a stroll, and it took on the appearance of a park in the 1800s as first the 144-foot-high Nelson's monument was erected, the impressive High Court building was raised at the western fringe of the Green, a timber theatre (Mumford's Penny Geggie) was built and the century's activity was capped when the People's Palace and Museum opened its doors for the first time in 1898.

For twenty-first-century Glaswegians probably the most significant link with the past came with the opening on the edge of the Green of everybody's favourite street market, the Barras, in 1923.

Moab McGonigal
Tent Churches of Europe, Victoria Park, Glasgow

Blowing a Gasket

What sort of thing makes the Scots really, really angry?

Miff Dudgeon
Southport, Lancashire

I'll tell you what makes the Scots really angry – just about anything you care to name.

They seem to me to be the most distraught, uptight people on the planet and their anger is a product of the Scottish whinge, the Caledonian cringe, the sense of injustice, the feeling of being hard done by, and this is very real and widespread. At the last count there were estimated to be some 320 different types of Scottish fury from road rage through checkout rage to the wrath of being surrounded by annoying people – and it seems to me that you Scots have the lot.

Mind you, if I was forced to live in a God-forsaken place like Scotland, with some of the ugliest women this side of Alpha Centauri and the most boorish males in Europe, then perhaps I too would put on an angry face. I once met a contented Scot but he was living in England, married to a Welsh girl and working for an Irish drinks company. I think that says it all.

If you ask by contrast what sort of thing makes folk in England angry, one cause might be the way Scottish publishers latch on to ideas which have their genesis south of the Border and produce a book which is a pale imitation of the original English work.

Rev. Roger Pedant
Bury St Edmunds, Suffolk

You can search the shelves of your local bookstore but you will not find another book – English or Scottish – which deals with Scottish issues in the manner of Does Anyone Like Midges? *— Ed.*

I get really, really angry by the way in which our Burns Night, a night for honest solidarity among ordinary Scots, has been appropriated by the pseudo-English. That gets me furious. Real Scots love the poetry of Robbie Burns but would rather chant three choruses of 'Land of Hope and Glory' than attend an event which has been hi-jacked by people who are basically sad individuals desperate for some sort of heritage – anybody's heritage.

In truth they are part-time Caledonians with double-barrel names, an English education and a warped sense of history. It is the ultimate irony that these folk, the fans of ceilidh kitsch, now dress in the garb of old Gaul, the tartan and trappings which their noble ancestors first tried to proscribe and then restored for their own entertainment. I feel totally justified in my anger. The very thought of it all makes one's blood boil!

Calum Hamilton-Menzies
Secretary, The Militant Socialist League, Upper East Dorm, Harrow Public School, London

New figures suggest that we Scots are getting angrier and angrier. Most of us now admit to getting angry at least once a day and women are apparently getting angrier than men, which at least is a nice wee change from them getting angrier with men!

The only consolation we can take from this depressing development is that we are not alone. The rest of Europe, indeed the world, seems to find it increasingly difficult to deal calmly with an ever more complex and testing society. So-called civilisation has sucked the calm from our souls.

But some of the wee trials that we face are totally unnecessary. Take, for example, this infuriating way in which TV commentators whether in sport or current affairs refer to England when they mean the United Kingdom. It's obviously built into the doon-sooth psyche. It's annoying, but no more than that.

As a matter of interest, a few years ago when I was completing my degree dissertation – Anger Management Amongst Cleansing Department Operatives in Brechin – at Strathtay University I carried out a survey of attitudes and came up with some interesting material, although I say it myself.

Most common causes of anger resulting in temper tantrums seem to be shopping, telephone sales, mobile phones, other people's temper tantrums, other people's children, moaners, the cost of living, poor results for your football team, shortage of money, unemployment, crime, being put down by others, being wrongly blamed for something or being talked about behind your back . . . Any of this familiar? Shall I continue? . . . being taken for granted, dirty streets, dog fouling, people who blow smoke into your face, spitting in the street, throwing away chewing gum, time-wasters such as workmen who don't turn up, irritating celebs like Jonathan Ross and Wayne Rooney, inconsiderate drivers, bad manners, self-satisfied radio presenters, loud music . . .

Not surprisingly, folk who put industrial waste in domestic bin bags were not popular amongst the cleansing department operatives. The list is endless. However, I would suggest that the folk in Brechin and the Scots in general are no more guilty than any other nationality of throwing a wobbler, of losing the plot and the heid at one and the same time. It's in the nature of things. Serenity is for gurus and saints. Bottling up anger is bad for the soul.

Willie Fury
The Needle, Provocation Row, Madashell, Surrey

Only a Rough Guide

I am planning to join a hunting party with my friends in the wilds of Scotland. How much about stags and hunting in the Scottish Highlands could I learn from the Book of Deer *and is it available in local bookshops?*

Frau Irma Gepäckträger
Hauptbahnhofstrasse 20, Frankfurt-am-Main, Germany

There is absolutely no point, Frau Gepäckträger, in acquiring a copy of the *Book of Deer* if you are heading for the Highlands to shoot some poor defenceless creature.

The *Book of Deer* is an illustrated manuscript which resurfaced in Cambridge University Library in 1860. It contains St John's Gospel and parts of Matthew, Mark and Luke. Scholars see it as historically important because of marginal notes in Gaelic dating from the eleventh and twelfth centuries referring to grants of land to an unnamed religious house, which is taken to be the Cistercian foundation of Deer Abbey, west of Peterhead in Aberdeenshire. There is nothing therein about agile, four-footed ruminants.

On second thoughts, perhaps the correspondent should find out a little more about the *Book of Deer* and about Scottish history in general before she arrives here, togged up for the kill. There are perhaps too many 'visitors' to this country who have neither knowledge nor concern for this country's heritage and see it, very much in the way that affluent Victorians did, as their private playground.

I know we need the tourist money but perhaps VisitScotland should consider a basic test for all visitors to Scotland which could be taken before arriving or before leaving Scotland. Failure to pass this simple quiz would result in an 'Ignorance Tax' to be collected on departure much in the same way as 'Airport Duty' is collected today.

Ewing Fearchar
Ballietoul Road House, Even Further Up the Glen,
Drumnadrochit, Inverness-shire

I rather think that Ewing Fearchar is being a bit unkind, indeed very unfair, to the German correspondent who had been asking for information about the *Book of Deer*.

If the truth be told, you'd be lucky to find a handful of Scots, even in the north-east, who have a scooby (sorry, clue) about the *Book of Deer*. There are people in Aberdeenshire who give the distinct impression that they've never seen a book, never mind having read one.

Rather than criticising other nationalities for their failings we should be encouraging study by our own people of such national treasures. The *Book of Deer*, generally regarded as one of Scotland's most significant early manuscripts, currently and confusingly housed in Cambridge University Library, is thought to have been written between AD 800 and AD 900 with the Gaelic additions which set down the Abbey's landholdings in Buchan dating from *c.* AD 1100. It can also be accessed on the internet.

The book was given to Cambridge as part of an eighteenth-century bequest and then lay forgotten for a century and a half. If devolution is to mean anything, this treasure should be back in Scottish hands – and smartish. My ancient university would be happy to provide a proper home for the work.

Emeritus Professor Silver Marjoribanks
Dept of Interesting Ideas, Memorial University of
Aberuthven, Perthshire

Something in the Air?

Can anyone tell me why crossing the invisible border from England into Scotland it is impossible to ignore the fact that you have moved into a different country?

Gordon Highroad
Shieling Number Six, Cathedral Street, Glasgow

Here we go again. Is it just me? Every so often we witness a balmy type of Northern Briton climbing out of the woodwork. This latest nonsense about sensing when you have crossed into Scotland just about takes the biscuit. Mr Highroad should be told that the 'Border' between Scotland and England is what it has always been, an artificial line drawn across the country from east to west or vice versa – an administrative convenience which crept backwards and forwards in an elastic style over the centuries to accommodate political expediency.

Is young Gordon – I presume he is young because no one with any sense of what the world is about could have made such a ridiculous suggestion – trying to say that the slurry or the exhaust fumes smell differently once you've crossed the Border (this totally artificial boundary), that in Scotland the grass is greener, the streams more sparkly and pure, the people more friendly, the wind less strident etc. etc.? What arrant nonsense. All boundaries are obstacles to balanced living. We are British, *sans frontiers*, and should be proud of it.

Felix Snark
MSP for the Posh Parts of Edinburgh,
The Upturned Boats, by Holyrood

The sensation of which Mr Highroad speaks is something which I have felt for years but been afraid to discuss openly for fear that people would think I had a screw loose.

In 1956 I left Scotland for the first time to attend a Boy Scout camp at Teignmouth in Devon. It was a long journey by rail to a part of Britain which felt like a foreign land. Don't get me wrong, the people were friendly enough, they were patient when we failed to pick up the dialect 'Oooohs' and 'Aaaahs' and the weather was simply glorious. It was a real experience.

However, the return rail journey was even more memorable. We crossed the Border and rattled on towards Beattock Summit. From the carriage window we stared at the hills and I was suddenly conscious of feeling as if I'd come 'home'. There was no obvious cause for this euphoria, the scenery and the day were unspectacular, but it was real enough – a feeling of well-being and ease.

Fifty years on I still have the same sensation when I'm arriving into the bustle of Edinburgh or Glasgow airports, alighting from the Zeebrugge ferry at Rosyth or making that cross-Border train journey again. None of these landfalls are scenically or intellectually inspiring but they surely represent a restoration of belonging.

Robert Louis Stevenson knew what we were on about. He wrote about returning to Scotland and finding 'life is warmer and closer; the hearth burns more redly; the lights of home shine softer on the rainy street; the very names, endeared in verse and music, cling nearer round our hearts.'

I'm pleased that this is all out in the open. I've bottled this sensation up for all those years suspecting I was a mad, closet Jacobite. Now that Mr Highroad has opened the door I hope that many others will admit to this joy of returning. It is, I think, a love of Scotland, or if you want to be pedantic, the idea of Scotland, untainted by political or intellectual considerations. It is straight from the heart.

Alec Kemp
Sunnybraes, Gretna

Can I offer a slightly different perspective on this debate? I live in Yorkshire but visit Scotland several times annually. On recrossing the Border to England I always feel a sense of deflation, a strange loss of something important. (No, my handbag hadn't been picked on Princes Street.) If I, as an Englishwoman, can feel this, then how much more emotional must the return of a Scot to his or her homeland from English soil be? You have something special in Scotland. Where can I sign up for Scottish citizenship?

Diane Wycherlie
Pit Props, Bingley, Yorkshire

Silence in Court!

Why are public displays of emotion and spontaneous applause totally prohibited during criminal trials in Scotland's High Court of Justiciary?

Professor Philippe Ragout
Department of Legal Niceties,
University of South Kamchatka

As a law student I always find it baffling that, when a jury returns a carefully considered verdict, the 'rules' dictate they shouldn't be applauded by the onlookers in the public gallery for the diligence they have shown in reaching a conclusion. We must also recognise that to a greater or lesser extent these restrictions apply in every court in the land.

I know all the arguments about the dignity and tradition of the court are well rehearsed but this is the twenty-first century and it seems the most natural thing in the world, particularly for the family of someone who has been attacked or robbed to show their relief that justice has been done. This is after all, when all is said and done, show business with a cast dressed up in wigs and cloaks like extras from Gilbert and Sullivan's *Iolanthe* strutting their stuff in front of the jury. Such performances cry out for a response. All that an overenthusiastic reaction will get you at present is a few hours cooling your heels in the courts cells and the possibility of a jail term for contempt of court.

Peter Pleader
The High Court of Justiciary, Jail Square,
Innellan, by Dunoon, Argyll

Even after being shown the door by the Scottish legal establishment for a minor indiscretion, I still believe that

Scotland has the best legal system in the world. To suggest that we should allow our courts to be transformed into variety theatres where each 'performance' is applauded is ridiculous. Where would you draw the line? Would whoops and cheers greet the closing speeches from counsel, or would the conclusion of evidence from a particularly convincing witness draw a round of applause and wild whistles? Would the judge's summing up prompt a Mexican wave or perhaps the passing above the heads of those in the public gallery of a huge flag bearing the motto of the Scottish Crown – *Nemo me impune lacessit*?

No, leave well alone. The legal establishment may be stuffed shirts but they hold a vital part of our national heritage in their hands and should always be treated with respect. They also, I should mention in closing, have the power to reinstate a lawyer who has respectfully served his punishment and is ready to eat humble pie.

Deloite Robery, former advocate (unjustly struck off for fraud)
Hill o' Beans, Plymouth, Montserrat

Ladies and gentlemen of the jury, the prosecution case . . . sorry, sorry, old habits die hard. I must say that the question of applause in court is an intriguing one. Over my years on the bench there were a number of instances of spontaneous applause from the public gallery which I came down heavily on. Dignity of the court and all that . . .

But I have to say, from the enlightened pastures of enforced retirement, I now take a totally different view. Let there be applause, cheering and general public involvement in the administration of justice. It's democratic, it's fun. Let the death penalty be reinstated and hanging, drawing and quartering given back its rightful place in our schedule of punishments. Capital punishment and public humiliation – that will cut the crime rate overnight.

Lord Tillydrone
c/o The Criterion Bar, Aberdeen

The Empire Strikes Back

Can you throw any light on the suggestion that the image of the heavy-bevvying Scot might originate in the activities of Roman spin doctors?

Caesar Glass
The Clachan, Glenlivet, Banffshire

We should realise that this is a slur visited not only on the Scots but also on the Welsh and the Irish, which in turn might give us a clue as to its origins. We must also consider whether it is really a myth. To discover why these Celtic peoples have been branded as heavy drinkers we must forget about their drinking as a response to bad weather, meaningless lifestyles and failure or (just occasionally) success on the football and rugby fields. The reasons are much older and more sinister. Roots of the image of the heavy-drinking Celt, I believe, may indeed date back almost 2,000 years to the days of the Roman Empire, when everyone outside that Empire was regarded as a barbarian and needed to be brought under the 'civilising' influence of Rome, either at the point of a sword or by more subtle means.

The Romans traded large quantities of wine with the Celtic tribes and this, apart from being a lucrative business, may also have been a clever way of undermining Celtic society. The Celts, incredibly, were reported to have drunk this wine in the same quantities as home-produced beer – their staple drink. Little wonder stories grew of drunken festivals in the halls of the Celtic chieftains. The damage was done, the hard-drinking Celt became a stereotype.

Professor Richard Derooth
Distillery, Ireland

Roman writer Marcellinus described the Celtic tribes as a race 'greedy for wine'. Where the myth may enter the equation is the assumption that all Celtic peoples behaved in this way. I would suggest that it is likely that the boozers were the aristocracy, where wine drinking performed a social function and may also have been seen as a power and prestige pastime – something exotic, foreign and expensive.

Sam Slammer
The Institute for Celtic Reality,
Druid Way, Cleethorpes, Lincs.

I am disappointed that you have seen fit to reopen this weary old saga about Roman involvement in creating the image of the heavy-drinking Scot. Out of the woodwork again will come all sorts of weirdos who see Rome as the evil empire. It will be suggested that the Celts were fed wine – a bit like the native Americans in the eighteenth and nineteenth centuries – in order to make them less of a threat and more pliable. What arrant nonsense! The Roman Empire was the most benevolent, civilising force in the history of the world. The simple truth is that the Scots like their drink but by and large cannot handle it.

The only real hope is that polite wine drinking as practised for millennia in the Mediterranean lands and more recently by Scotland's thinking classes spreads to the unwashed masses – and the sooner the better.

Julius Agricola McClung
Ninth Legion Re-enactment Group,
Roman Road, Bearsden, Glasgow

If, like me, you live in Hammerfest, the most northerly town in Europe, you would realise that all of us in the northern lands need some comfort through eleven and a half months of winter. We simply like our beer up here, just as the Scots do. It seems rather harsh to blame the Roman Empire. After all, I hear they built some really good roads and knew how to throw a party.

Per Feroth
Proprietor, Last Chance Saloon,
Main Street, Hammerfest, Norway

All evidence suggests that life for the ordinary Celtic farmers in Gaul and Britain consisted of a punishing daily work routine on the land, which didn't change much until the agricultural revolution of the 1700s and 1800s and left little time for heavy or regular drinking.

But so-called binge drinking, a trait often identified with the Celtic descendants, becomes more comprehensible if we appreciate that during lean years when grain was in short supply the majority of the harvest was consumed as a foodstuff rather than for brewing. Naturally, when there was a sufficiency, drinking, particularly in the dark winter months, took on an urgent flavour. Examining the reports of classical authors, it is not so much an affinity for strong drink which we encounter but an inability to handle wine sensibly.

It seems possible that the Romans, and Mediterranean folk generally, with their steady daily consumption were, in fact, drinking proportionately more than the Celts and might still do so. Scholars tend now to think that the Celts were not riotous drinkers but that the nobles had become exposed to a drinking tradition that was not their own and which they handled badly.

It does appear that the classical sources are misleading or at least selective. They had probably witnessed drinking at important warrior feasts. It has to be admitted that there was a liking among the Celts for drink but Roman PR spin unfairly plastered the ordinary hard-working Celt with a boozy brush which really applied to their wine-guzzling leaders. The London-based media has been happy to swallow and regurgitate this Roman propaganda ever since. Let the people drink, I say.

Sir Walter E. E. Beveridge
Chairman, Mid-Caledonian Brewers, Raploch, Stirling

Gaelic, No Way

Why do Orkney and Shetland get Gaelic programmes when only a handful of folk in the Northern Isles speak or even care about the language?

Therolf Hairsplitter
1 Stavanger Close, Burray, Orkney

The first point that needs to be made in response to Mr Hairsplitter's inquiry is that Scotland is an ethnically diverse nation influenced in its formative years by several cultures, two of the most important being Gaelic and Norse. Sadly the old Norn dialect has been largely allowed to fade away.

Gaelic was a national language of Scotland (and last time I checked Orkney and Shetland, like it or not, are part of Scotland) after the expansionist Gaels swallowed Pictland and remained so until it gave way under socio-political pressures to Lowland Scots.

The importance of Gaelic is without question. As one of the four surviving Celtic languages it is surely one of our most significant cultural assets. Both the BBC and the independent television networks have a public obligation to help spread the message. Anyone with a sense of history must understand the importance of promoting Gaelic in Scotland, just as Norn should have been and as Lowland Scots and Doric hopefully will be increasingly.

Only by continuing to highlight Gaelic and the work being done to sustain the language in the media will that important part of our heritage realign itself to the modern world. Now, this approach is not going to please everyone but the truth is that television companies are turning out some fascinating documentaries and current affairs programmes in Gaelic and generally these are subtitled. So, there are no excuses for not learning about the place of Gaelic and Gaelic culture in the modern world.

Hakon Haakon
343 St Magnus Lane, Kirkwall, Orkney

Is anyone surprised that the Northern Isles have Gaelic television foisted on them when they would rather watch tartan paint dry? This is part of a great long-running conspiracy to marginalise the Norse islands of Orkney and Shetland, which only came under Scottish sway in 1468. It took Orkney Rugby Club umpteen years to be allowed to play in the national leagues because of our supposed 'remoteness'.

This daft promotion of the language in totally non-Gaelic speaking areas such as Orkney and Shetland can also lead to some strange twists. I read that a few years ago the only Gaelic speakers in Orkney were a family of Chinese restaurant owners who had learned Gaelic while working in Stornoway.

Gaelic, along wi' Doric and Lowland Scots, is a toy of the chattering classes of Scotland, a plaything for folk wi' mair time on their hands than is good for them. It is trendy and cool to support lost causes like this. As far as Orkney and Shetland are concerned, the Scottish Executive should learn that we don't spake Gaelic roon' here!

Cathal Carstairs
Flat 4, The Chambered Tomb, Papa Stour, Shetland

8
Toil and tragedy

⊙ More Questions than Answers

What on earth is this 'West Lothian Question' on which the whole future of the United Kingdom appears to hang?

Glen Gyle
Wendy's Pizza Parlour,
20001 West 46th Street, Washington DC, USA

Well, this is neither doubt over whether Livingston FC will bounce back immediately to the Premier League after relegation, nor yet whether aubergines or courgettes are the best buy in the Bathgate superstores. No, the West Lothian Question has been described as the ultimate parliamentary enigma, a classic political paradox, an epic riddle and the question with no answer. In the past year it has taken on the proportions of *The Da Vinci Code* in its complexity and things, I fear, are likely to get worse before they get better.

The problem has arisen from the establishment of the devolved Scottish Parliament in Edinburgh and the fact that Scottish Members of Parliament still at Westminster have, since then, been voting occasionally on purely English matters.

This has delighted Tony Blair – who has regularly relied on these votes of Scots Labour MPs to carry the day when contentious legislation affected England – but has angered others, notably the Tories, who see the whole business as a negation of democracy.

The problems which might arise on voting rights under a devolved system of government were first raised by West Lothian MP Tam Dalyell in 1972. Thereafter it has been universally known as 'The West Lothian Question'.

Dominic Ramsay
Dean of the Faculty of Law, Ramsbutt University,
Half-Fried, New Mexico, USA

The whole West Lothian Question is irrelevant. When we Tories take control in Scotland again, the devolution machine will be put in reverse.

Felix Snark
MSP for the Posh Parts of Edinburgh,
The Upturned Boats, by Holyrood

Whenever I hear the West Lothian Question mentioned I can't help thinking of all the complex political situations with seemingly no solution which have arisen over the centuries. Take for instance a mind-boggingly complicated financial negotiation in the nineteenth century known to history as the Schleswig-Holstein Question. It used to be said that only three people knew the answer to the Question: one had forgotten it, the second had gone mad trying to work out a solution and a third knew the answer but found it impossible to explain. The West Lothian Question is a bit like that, I fear. Most situations have a solution and, those that don't, time resolves.

Speir Askew
Emeritus Professor, The Institute for the Study of
Unanswerable Questions, The Potting Shed, Lanarkshire

The whole West Lothian Question is irrelevant. When the green agenda comes to the fore, the only question worth asking will be how many acres of organic broccoli can be grown in West Lothian?

Letitia Marrow
Smokey Bottom, Ilfracombe, Devon

The whole West Lothian Question is irrelevant. When we take control in Scotland after independence, the 'English' parliament will have all the time in the world to see to their own affairs.

Mendip McCurd
The Sheiling, 1314 Gallowgate, Glasgow

If you listened to the professional commentators you might imagine that there is no solution to the West Lothian Question. Not so. It might be possible to set up an English Grand Committee to deal with exclusively English business, Scottish MPs might abstain from voting in all business that does not affect Scotland, or Scottish MPs might absent themselves completely from Westminster. Most folk believe that the latter would preface the repeal of the Act of Union while the other 'solutions' present various problems which political parties find difficult to address. But to say this is the question with no answer is simply nonsense. Where there's a will and all that . . .

Captain Ernest Gravel
Cultural Counsellor, The British Embassy,
Palindrome, Rubovia

The whole West Lothian Question is irrelevant. When we take control of the means of production in Scotland, all MSPs and MPs will be hung, drawn and quartered in St Andrew Square. Nae question aboot it!

Dan McLean
Mick McGahey House, Clartyhole Mews, Dumbarton

Them Thar Hills

Has Scotland ever had a 'gold rush'?

P. A. N. Handel
The Diggings, Keefer, Sutherland

The only Scottish gold rush that really merits such a name would be the outstanding performance of the Scottish swimming team in Melbourne at the 2006 Commonwealth Games but, historically, I presume the event Mr Handel is referring to was the discovery of gold at Kildonan in Sutherland in 1869. This caused quite a stir at the time, with predictions of a North Sea oil-style bonanza for the Highland counties but it quickly became clear that the gold would be in insufficient quantities to make mining profitable.

Terry Trench
14 Archerfield Avenue, Peterhead, Aberdeenshire

Despite his surname, Dangerous Dan McGrew was not overtly Scottish nor does Scotland offer many valid comparisons with the Klondike. However, the possibility that somewhere in Scotland there was enough gold to prompt a 'rush' always interested our Scottish kings.

At the beginning of the sixteenth century James IV had a mining operation at Crawford Muir in Lanarkshire where the chief of the enterprise was a Sir James Pettigrew, ably assisted by a team of European engineers. This enterprise, along with the rest of the Scottish nation, ground to a halt after Flodden in 1513, although by 1526 we find a company of Germans being granted the privilege of searching Scotland for gold mines. Since then, foreign entrepreneurs seeking gold are found in the public record but we can assume that ordinary folk were always on the lookout for gold. Even into the current era, companies have been searching the hills for gold.

It is generally accepted that the Kildonan 'fever' of 1869 was the nearest thing to a Scottish Klondike. It has most assuredly gained a niche in Highland folklore. At any one time during that year up to 400 gold panners could be found along the strath – not only local men but experienced gold miners from Australia and North America. It was one such émigré Scot, Helmsdale-born Robert Gilchrist, who sparked off events in Kildonan in 1868 when, after seventeen years spent in the Australian goldfields, he returned home and started to turn up gold in the tributaries of the Helmsdale River, the best sources being the Kildonan and Suisgil burns. Excitement was heightened by the discovery of a gold nugget weighing in at over two ounces which, surprise, surprise, found its way into the possession of the Duke of Sutherland.

Edwin Sapper
The Gold Diggers' Rest Home, 14 Robert Service Avenue, Riverbed, Yukon, Canada

Lament for the Clyde

Did the world-renowned Scottish commercial shipbuilding industry really have to die?

Tony Welding
Osaka, Japan

It is a remarkable fact that when the Clydeside shipbuilding industry was at its peak more than 100,000 people made their way to work every morning through the huge wooden gates in places like Govan, Clydebank and Port Glasgow. It was an industry respected throughout the world which produced the greatest warships and ocean liners ever seen – and it seemed invincible.

Generations of shipyard workers could never have imagined the industry would decline as rapidly as it did in the 1970s. A huge worldwide market was lost in just a couple of decades. A very special breed of men – riveters, welders, draughtsmen, engineers, joiners and plumbers – had evolved in the hundred years since large-scale industrial shipbuilding began on the Clyde and within a few years the industry had imploded. Defence orders today constitute what work remains.

However, even in its death throes, the Scottish commercial shipbuilding industry – through the famous Upper Clyde Shipbuilders work-in during the early 1970s – provided a focus for protest against the dismantling of the Scottish economy and the rights of the Scottish people to have a say in their own destiny. In the decades since that crash it has often been asked if the contraction of Scottish shipbuilding was inevitable. Blame has been laid at the door of the workers and their trade unions for lack of flexibility and laziness as well as at the door of management and government for their failure to anticipate improvements needed in an ever-more sophisticated industry. These improvements were essential given the dramatic changes post-war in world shipbuilding, particularly as defeated Japan entered the industry.

You would expect me to say this, but, on balance, the bulk of the blame must surely lie with Government who failed to come up with an investment programme. As early as the 1950s some Clydeside workers were beginning to sense that their industry was doomed.

People tend to forget that the construction of a great ship is a co-operation of industry, science and art. At one and the same time you are creating a thing of beauty and a marvellous piece of engineering. The shipyards had their own character and created and sustained communities which, when the yards began to run down and eventually close, were torn apart and scattered to the winds. Stacking shelves in supermarkets or serving burgers in a fast food restaurant can never create solidarity and a sense of belonging among ordinary folk in the way that shipbuilding did. Could the industry have been saved? Perhaps – but complacency at all levels was undoubtedly the killer.

Ted Bridge
Former welder and shop steward, John Brown's Shipyard, Clydebank

If you look at the way other nations managed to adapt to the changed circumstances in the aftermath of World War II it seems distinctly possible that a sizeable commercial shipbuilding industry could have survived on the Clyde. After all, such ships are still being built all over the world.

'Niche market' is the current buzzword but that was

precisely what shipbuilding in this country needed to identify. All the skills were available on Clydeside; really what management needed to do was to upgrade the yards and identify a suitable product.

Instead of doing the work on what Jimmy Reid, the Upper Clyde Shipbuilders work-in leader in 1971, has called 'vast hulks', which could have been left to Third World yards, the Clyde yards could and probably should have gone for more sophisticated, specialist markets, such as small cruise liners.

The argument that cheap labour outside Europe would inevitably have killed off the bulk of the Scottish industry, even with improvement, is questionable.

Dr Ramsay Keel
School for the Study of What Might Have Been,
Mombassa, Kenya

Jamie's Dread

From what I've read of King James VI of Scotland (I of England), he strikes me as a very nervous and insecure individual. I've seen it suggested that he was obsessed with the idea that he would be assassinated. Is this accurate?

C. E. L. J. C. S. S. M. Stuart
Killer's Lane, Clydebank, West Dunbartonshire

There does indeed seem to be something to this story, Mr Stuart. The speed and enthusiasm with which James packed his bags at Holyrood and abandoned Scotland to take the throne of England on the death of Elizabeth I in 1603 would inevitably make him nervous about any return to Scotland.

The Gowrie Conspiracy in 1600, when James, in the middle of a hunting expedition, appears to have been enticed by the Ruthven family into Gowrie House in Perth, may have been the source of his paranoia. Although the incident, which saw the principal Ruthvens slain, was believed by some to have been engineered by the king to get rid of dangerous opponents, current academic thinking is that he had indeed faced an assassination plot. In the late 1500s he had also been harassed by Francis Stuart, the Earl of Bothwell, who was even accused of recruiting the witches of North Berwick to help scupper the king.

Add to this the great resentment there was in many quarters in England over his accession then you begin to see why James was a wee bit jumpy.

Hillary Gore
2, rue des Martyrs, Coup de Grâce, Guadeloupe

There can be no doubt that James was worried about his security. His state visit to Scotland in 1617 includes two telling incidents which suggest, at the very least, that he was on his guard. At Dumfries he was served a dish of vendace, or freshwater herring, but was so offended by the smell that he leapt to his feet shouting 'Treason!', presumably because he thought he was about to be poisoned. On the other side of the country he visited Sir George Bruce's high-tech coal mine off Culross. A caisson had been built at the low water line and a shaft dug down to the coal seam which was then worked out under the river for about a mile. James and his party entered the mine from the shore but, when they surfaced in the artificial islet, surrounded by water, James panicked and again 'began to shout of treason as loud as he could bawl'.

The evidence would seem to confirm that he was constantly in fear of his life but whether this had reached the stage of an obsession is more difficult to assess.

Lionel Lynch
Curator, the James VI Experience, The Shambles, Hemel Hempstead, Herts.

No Beach Holiday

My fellow courier Hamish says that thousands of Jacobite prisoners were transported to camps in the Balearic Islands after the 1715 and 1745 Uprisings. Is this true?

Flora Grant
Hedonistic Holidays, Arenal, Majorca, Spain

I have a feeling that your colleague is getting a bit mixed up with his or her exotic islands. What is true is that some modern tourist Meccas did figure as destinations for Jacobite prisoners. After both the 1715 and 1745 Jacobite risings, hundreds of Scots, not thousands as is often claimed, were sentenced to transportation to the British colonies in the Caribbean – certainly not to the Mediterranean.

Rather than to camps, they found their way to sugar and tobacco plantations where, it has to be said, conditions were slightly less comfortable than at Club Med. In 1716, after the rising had been quelled, 639 Jacobite prisoners were conveyed to the sugar islands in the British West Indies and to the southern colonies in America. It is known that 145 reached the West Indies and may at a later date have moved on to the American mainland colonies. Six ships brought 451 prisoners to Maryland, Virginia and South Carolina. The remaining 45 died on passage.

It is thought that eventually many of those deported after the '15 found their way back illegally to the Scottish Highlands. This was seen as a major problem and after the '45, in order to prevent a reoccurrence, the Crown solicitor even suggested that the Jacobite prisoners should be branded to discourage them from returning. Up to 1,000 prisoners were sentenced to transportation but only some 600 actually sailed. Once again they were heading principally for the modern holiday islands of Jamaica and Barbados.

In fact, very few are reported to have returned on the latter occasion, which suggests they realised that the Stuart cause was lost forever.

Dermot Dorcas
Association for Victims of Hanoverian Oppression,
14 Garscube Road, Glasgow

Camped Beside a Good Thing

Why did Scottish emigrants to North America in particular seem to consistently punch above their weight in the New World?

Leven Strauss
Tour Guide, Level 42, The Grand Canyon, Colorado, USA

For the entire nineteenth century and a large part of the twentieth, Scotland exported her sons and daughters in substantial numbers. Throughout the period from the end of the Napoleonic Wars in 1815 through to the inter-war years, 1919–39, it has been estimated that some 44 million people left Europe in what historians have described as mankind's greatest ever exodus. The Scottish contribution to this great haemorrhage was perhaps around 2 million, seemingly a small element in the overall picture. However, when you consider the proportionate loss of people then we begin to shoot up the emigration league table. Scotland was, and remains, a small nation which can ill afford to lose young, talented people – but she did, in large numbers.

A point worth making in relation to the *Lochaber No More* scenario of forced exile, most poignantly focused in the Clearances, is that it conveys the impression that Scots were either chased or squeezed out of their home ground. Of course, this was often true in the Western Highlands. However, although Scots were cleared from the land, exiled as political, military or religious prisoners, indentured for long periods as servants, most made their own life choice and decided to risk the dangerous sea voyages and the uncertainties of new worlds in order to make a better life for themselves and their families.

It often seems that the great Scottish legions who emigrated were overachievers. If this is correct, why did it happen? It is really impossible to gauge, in anything other than general terms, the depth and width of the contribution of these Scots to the emerging countries of the New World in the 1800s. I will resist the temptation to provide long charts of Carnegie-style achievement in the old Commonwealth and the USA – presidential lists, business entrepreneurs, military leaders etc. The biographical dictionaries are packed with Scots. However, when you think about it, these praise works offer no insights unless set for proper comparison against the performance and impact of other ethnic groups. To be honest, comparative contributions are just about unquantifiable, although the other ethnic groups, I have discovered, also understandably, have a high opinion of their contribution to the new lands.

Anton Deck
Birlinghouse Stockbrokers, Toronto, Canada

The received wisdom from the academics is that the Scots did perform well. There is a wealth of the aforementioned praise literature about Scots' achievement, particularly in North America. Why should this be so? Well, the Scots had the advantage of coming from a culture where a broad-based education was valued and, just as significantly, where publishing was an established business. One scholar suggests that, faced in the later nineteenth century with an influx of immigrants from southern and eastern Europe, people of Scots or Ulster-Scots descent began in their writing vigorously to champion the role their ancestors had played.

Having English as their native tongue gave Scots a head start in settling Canada and the United States. Psychologically, the Scots would have been more at home than the later arriving Europeans. The twentieth-century catchword 'networking' sums up the way the Scots benefited from a framework of Scots interest groups. I have heard this network described as the Scottish Mafia, an almost Masonic-like brotherhood, which included in its community of interest St Andrew's, Caledonian, Highland and Burns clubs.

The story of the great Scottish exodus is a remarkable one and, as it becomes an ever more popular subject for study with the growth of family history and genealogy groups, more and more tales of the Caledonian emigrants are certain to emerge.

Dan Boone
Possum Protection League,
Cripple Creek, Tennessee, USA

All the Fun . . .

Where is the Glasgow Fair held and how many people usually attend?

Alec Holliday
Silver Sands Motel, The Esplanade, Miami, Florida, USA

Oh dear! The Glasgow Fair is actually the annual two-week break enjoyed by Glaswegians in July – a time past when the city came to a halt. On Fair Friday in Glasgow tools were downed and the great factory and shipyard gates were locked fast. Like cheerful sardines, tens of thousands of holidaymakers (mostly men, the women were busy packing the bags) crowded every available bar space, often spilling out into the street in their jubilation – by the following morning Glasgow was a strangely quiet place.

That this is an ancient tradition is not in dispute – some experts believe the Glasgow Fair dates back eight centuries to the Middle Ages – but it effectively disappeared by the mid 1960s, changed forever by cheaper travel, more flexible holidays, a population drift away from the old heart of Glasgow and the decline of city-based heavy industry.

It is interesting to recall that this shutdown was welcomed by the managers in the West of Scotland's heavy industries. It was a time, with production suspended, when vital plant maintenance could be carried out, special holiday squads crawling through the dark interiors of the boilers, scraping them clean and performing 101 other vital tasks.

Billy Thom
Fun in the Sun Holidays,
West Nile Street, Glasgow

There was indeed a genuine Glasgow Fair which gave its name to the city holiday. The fair used to be held in front of the Cathedral but, by the early 1800s, had moved to Glasgow Green. 'Glesga Fair is noo open,' the red-coated bellman would shout at the Cross. Way back in the Celtic twilight a formula was devised for determining the exact date of Glasgow Fair Monday which in turn shaped the holiday. It was always to be the first Monday after the second Saturday in July. And there were strange traditions. Old hacks would tell you that on the Saturday of the Glasgow Fair the wonderfully named Paps of Jura in the Hebrides were always visible from the city's West End.

It's suggested that the saying 'Doon the Watter' originated with the Glasgow Fair during the 1800s as folk crowded the Clyde steamers but no one I've spoken to ever heard the phrase used – except in the city newspapers which, right into the late 1900s, seemed obsessed with having a Glasgow Fair holiday story whether one was justified or not.

People actually get very nostalgic about the Fair but it is best to keep the memories in perspective. As often as not, instead of sunshine, low cloud and smog made it impossible to see the West End from the city centre and, on the famous Clyde steamers, passengers were frequently drenched by downpours and made nauseous by the rolling swell. But it was the Fair. If we are to believe the stories we read of global warming and the Mediterranean resorts destined to have scorchingly dry, Saharan summers then perhaps the Glasgow Fair will undergo a renaissance. All we have to do now is discover a new generation of cheery landladies.

Oscar Fund
Shangri-La, Easterhouse Road, Glasgow

The outside world was always delighted at the prospect of the great Glasgow exodus. As city columnist William Hunter once wrote: 'Other places knew they were coming. Rothesay boatmen rubbed their hands at the prospect. Blackpool barmen had a gleam in their eye. And every July the Isle of Man sank another inch or so under the stampede of dancing Glasgow feet' — Ed.

Pit of Despond

I have seen vague references to the atrocious conditions under which Scottish children were expected to work in the country's mines during the early years of the Industrial Revolution. Was it really so bad and why did no one step in to halt this?

Dan Deep
Salisbury Way, Aberystwyth, Wales

It could be argued that over the centuries, apart altogether from the dangers of their employment, Scotland's miners, particularly in the coal industry, were the most put-upon working-class group in the land. These people had little or no liberty and could be moved about at the whim of the coal master. In the early 1700s, in legislation which smacked of medieval practice, runaway serfs – because in reality that was their status – were to be returned to their master providing eight years had not passed since they absconded. Effectively the miner and his family were tied to the coalmaster for life.

This situation lasted until the late 1700s when this criminal system was swept away by Acts of 1775 and 1799. However, for the children, as the Industrial Revolution dawned, it remained a miserable life. They lived the twilight existence of cave dwellers, often being asked to undertake heavy jobs with which adults would have struggled. Only with a growing public awareness of the dreadful conditions under which the miners – and particularly their children – were expected to work were improvements introduced as the century progressed. It is hardly a surprise then that miners had such a strong voice in the early labour movement in Scotland.

Bing Wallsend (the ghost of, aged twelve)
Cubicle 6, Old Pithead Baths, Monktonhall Colliery

Scotland has much of which to be proud in her history but the terrible abuse of children who worked in the nation's collieries in the first half of the nineteenth century will remain forever a blot on our reputation. Horrific evidence of the use of children in the mines came to light during the work of a Royal Commission which gathered evidence in 1842. The facts which the commission pulled together shocked the gentlefolk, some of whom simply refused to believe what they were being told.

In West Lothian a quarter of the workforce in the mines – boys and girls – were found to be under the age of thirteen; in the West of Scotland a slightly more enlightened regime seemed to have prevailed and only boys were permitted into the pits. The working day could last up to thirteen hours. There were no meal breaks and cold food had to be snatched whenever the opportunity arose. The commission heard that these boys would often start work at the age of eight as 'trappers' who opened and shut the underground gates to allow people or coal to pass; at the age of ten they became 'quarter men', allowed to draw their father's coal from the face to the pit shaft; by the age of sixteen they could be wielding a pick.

In the East of Scotland, girls worked alongside the boys

and, with the women, moved most of the coal underground. At the age of six or seven they could face a fourteen-hour day. Some carried half-hundredweight loads at the age of six! By the age of sixteen some were carrying two-hundredweight loads of coal. Others pushed and pulled heavy carts in cramped, damp and dangerous conditions. Fatalities from crushing injuries were common. Long-term illness was endemic.

An eleven-year-old girl told how she started work at Loanhead Colliery, near Falkirk, at 2 a.m. each morning, bringing coal to the surface by means of ladders. Twenty journeys were needed and she worked until 2 p.m. – a twelve-hour shift. Another girl said she often worked a twenty-four-hour shift, rested for two hours and then went straight back down for another twelve-hour shift.

Worst of all, it is reported that, without education, the mine children developed 'hellish dispositions' and were sadly ignorant. A little boy from Tranent, East Lothian, nine miles from Scotland's capital, said he had no idea where Edinburgh was. In Fife the miners and their families were so detested that they were refused permission to be buried in consecrated ground.

Peter 'The Pick' Gilroy
Airbles Road, Motherwell, Lanarkshire

Merely Big Weans?

Why do grown Scotsmen (and women) feel the need to re-enact our bloody battles? Is it not better that these sorry events remain in the history books?

Fergus Fechter
22 Artillery Way, Aldershot, Yorkshire

There is a slogan used by re-enactment groups in the United States – 'Spend your weekends somewhere really different – the seventeenth century'. That just about sums up the appeal, indeed *joy*, of being involved in re-enactment groups for hundreds of Scots and thousands of folk the world over. It is a chance to see the world as it once was.

There seems to be an impression that anyone who takes part in enacting famous battles and campaigns from Scottish history must be missing a slate or is clearly a latent psychopath. The truth is that we are neither.

Our shared delight is a love of our nation's incredible history and a strong desire to learn more about it, not just by reading books but by trying to recreate the experience. Although re-enactors will stage a town fair, a knightly tournament, a coronation or other ceremonial events, it is in the mock battles, I believe, that we come nearest to the genuine experiences of a previous age.

It is not our desire to be involved in violence for the fun of it, but an attempt to understand how it actually felt to line up on the field of battle, to face the serried ranks of the enemy, to defend your country at a time when you met your enemy in hand-to-hand combat rather than in a laser-guided missile exchange.

Nor are we wannabe territorial army soldiers in fancy dress, running around boggy fields banging each other over the napper with pikes, as has been claimed. It is not our goal to hurt the opposition – they are seeking the same experience as we are, but the more realistic we can make a replayed Culloden, Flodden, Bannockburn or Dunbar, the more authentic the experience.

With the last of these epoch-making battles, the hope of

myself and my brother Covenanters is that in the rerun we might yet get a victory!

Trooper Maxie Todd
Red Hackle Covenanters, Dalmellington, Ayrshire

What *is* that old git Fechter moaning about? Warfare is the thing to keep the kids off the streets and away from drugs and unbridled sex. Not everyone can join the real army – not everyone wants to join the real army – but this re-enactment lark allows young folk to get a bit of aggression out of their systems with only the incidental chance of somebody getting hurt.

He also forgets that charity re-enactments raise tens of thousands of pounds annually for worthy organisations such as Barnardo's and Leukaemia Research.

Actually, rather than trimming back the number of mock battles that take place I would like to suggest a dramatic expansion in the number and range of battles and skirmishes that are restaged. How about the clashes between the Glasgow razor gangs of the 1930s or the re-enactment of skirmishes during the Crofters War in the late 1800s? There are all sorts of possibilities.

Hans Mölke
Betty Davis Drive, Kirriemuir

It makes my heart glad to see folk jumping to the defence of re-enactment groups whether they are restaging Bannockburn or the Normandy landings. We should be proud as punch of our Scottish military heritage and such organisations help remind the nation at large of our wonderful achievements on the battlefield.

Just as, each year at Up-Helly-Aa, the Guizer Jarl takes on the persona of a leading Norse adventurer, why shouldn't re-enactors take on the roles of Bruce, Wallace, Sir James Douglas, Bonnie Prince Charlie? We should remember that such re-enactments have a distinguished pedigree. Medieval re-enactments often featured themes from the days of the Roman Empire.

One trend which I find particularly distressing is the increasing opportunity given to women and children to play roles in the fighting. It never happened in reality and we should not allow political correctness to change the reality of history. If they want to re-enact let them do the cooking or wash the bloodstained battle garments or show us how to thatch their hovel. This politically correct trend to downgrade actual conflict in favour of social history has changed the re-enactment movement in the United States. Let it not happen in Scotland. There may well be a vocal antiwar lobby in most countries these days but they must not be allowed to spoil the enjoyment of thousands who want to join battle.

Ranald Burgoyne-Tosh (Lt Col. Rtd)
West Perthshire Yeomanry, Battlefield House, Kenmore

The Other James Braid

I am an enthusiastic golfer and I know that James Braid was a famous Open champion in the early 1900s. Now, my psychologist tells me that there was another James Braid who coined the word 'hypnosis'. Can anyone tell me more of this mystery man?

Duff Green
The Caddie's Hut, The Old Course, Milnathort,
Kinross-shire

This is one of the most remarkable, largely untold stories of Scottish medical history and we owe so much to the other James Braid, it's time his story was better known. I am happy to enlighten Mr Green. James Braid the golfer won the Open five times between 1901 and 1910 but we need to go back a couple of generations to find the other James Braid, also a Fifer. I know of no immediate family link between the two men but Fife is still stowed out with Braids so if there is one, I'm sure they'll tell me.

James Braid, the doctor, studied medicine at Edinburgh University before going into general practice and being persuaded south to practise in Manchester. It was there in 1841 that he attended a demonstration by an exponent of mesmerism; truthfully, it was more of a variety show, with people being put into a trance and persuaded to do the oddest things, such as lapping milk out of a dog's bowl.

Braid was convinced that what he had seen was mainly collusion or illusion or a bit of both, but the possibility of a trance-like state fascinated him. These were dangerous waters into which he was dipping his toe. The medical establishment simply refused to believe it was anything but trickery or theatricals and would cry sorcery at any call for closer study of the phenomenon. This dogmatic approach reached the ludicrous stage when a man had his leg amputated while in this strange trance and an eminent physiologist declared that he had been simply pretending not to feel the pain.

Mind you, the reasons for the blind rejection of this phenomenon are obvious in retrospect – some of the effects of hypnotism do seem magical. It was believed to induce clairvoyance and there is evidence to suggest that it does precisely that. For example, patients can 'see' objects out of their vision while under a trance.

James Braid, described by friends and acquaintances as a down-to-earth, cheery individual, left that meeting in 1841 to begin his life's work. He found by experiment that the trance state was real enough and that it could be induced simply by fixing the patient's attention on an inanimate object. This brought on what was described as 'abnormal, nervous sleep'. Originally he called it somnambulism but settled for 'neuro-hypnotism', shortened to hypnotism, a word he coined in 1843.

According to his biographers, he plugged away at his research with meticulous care and good-humoured persistency until the German and French mind doctors began to adopt his approach and by the 1880s many had incorporated hypnotism into their treatment of nervous disorders.

Pablo de Navarre
Council of World Brain Watchers, Langholm

Science and mankind generally owe an enormous debt to James Braid, the man responsible for pinning down the phenomenon of hypnosis. I think it's fair to say that the nature of hypnotism is still a great mystery to this day, although what is clear is that your everyday self can go walkabout under hypnosis, to be replaced by an extraordinarily biddable alter ego. I know: I use the technique three nights weekly and twice on Saturdays to large and enthusiastic audiences.

The Great Hypnotico
c/o The Beach Ballroom, Troon, Ayrshire

⟨⟩ A Close Encounter

My grandmother, towards the end of her life, kept recalling Glasgow's 'wally' closes. Was this senility or what?

Herbert Goff
Mexican Hat, Utah, USA

It seems unlikely that Mr Goff will have a copy of the *Concise Scots Dictionary* handy in the exotic surroundings of Mexican Hat but if he did, he would discover that the word 'wally', 'wallie' or 'waly' has a fascinating and varied pedigree.

As well as meaning 'pleasant' or 'sturdy', the word refers most commonly to glazed porcelain or china. It is probably most often heard in the context of ornamental china dogs, or 'wally dugs'. Most homes had a pair of these mutts on the mantelpiece. There might be a 'wally sink' in your tenement room and kitchen and, for sure, your grandfather and/or grandmother would keep their 'wallies', their false teeth, in a tumbler of water by the bedside.

The wally (my own choice of spelling) close was a notable feature of the Glasgow tenement scene into the middle of last century and, for those lucky enough still to live in a restored and decorated wally close, the smart, glazed tiles surely brighten their existence to this day. I feel quite certain that your mother, Mr Goff, would have been very proud of her wally close and kept it spotlessly clean. Plain white tiles were most common.

Between the 1880s and the start of the First World War, the first batch of Glasgow tenements built in the early nineteenth century, which had become overcrowded, badly lit, cold, rat-infested, disease-plagued slums, were demolished and an intense phase of new tenement building took place.

This is the period when the decorated closes made their appearance.

Hector Gilbert
Tenement Dwellers Monthly, Sauchiehall Street, Glasgow

One important aspect of the introduction of fancy, decorated tiles into Glasgow housing which Mr Gilbert appears to have overlooked is the fact that the condition of the older tenements so shocked social campaigners that there was a determination to make the new tenement properties as sanitary as possible. It was clear that tiles would be easy to keep clean and therefore were introduced primarily as a health option rather than as some sort of innovative artistic experiment. As far as I understand, despite the fact that Glasgow had an active pottery industry in the first decades of the twentieth century, most of the tiles used in the city came from the south, probably from Staffordshire.

Cecil McCann
Moffat, Dumfriesshire

As a newspaper reporter in Glasgow in the 1940s and 1950s I had more occasion than most while on duty to observe the wally closes of the city and the splendid tile displays found there. Surprisingly, perhaps, many of the most striking tile displays were in closes in the run-down parts of the city. Closes played a big part in my life as a calls reporter (paying regular visits to police, ambulance and fire stations in the quest for stories). In the trade, persuading the news desk to get shot of a story which was causing more bother than it was worth came to be known as 'shoving it up a close' – wally or otherwise! In addition, one of the great unsolved mysteries of Glasgow journalism in the twentieth century was the fact that, when covering a story where the main protagonists lived up a tenement close, the people you were seeking always seemed to live on the top floor whether the building was three, four or five storeys high. Uncanny, it was. And, remember, there were no lifts in those days!

Andrew 'Scoop' McKellar
Mitchell Street, Glasgow

Last Rites

There still seems to be an undercurrent of dismay that the traditional Scottish Sunday is disappearing. Football is played, public houses fling their doors wide, shops now go like a fair and trains, boats and planes operate on the Sabbath. But what exactly are we are supposed to be losing? I wish someone would explain.

Tim Gusman
Eastcote Avenue, Forfar

The short answer to Mr Gusman's query is that we are not losing a great deal. The truth surely is that the vast majority of Scottish churchgoers over past centuries attended the Kirk and the other Christian denominations as a duty, a family obligation and because to do otherwise would be seen to be eccentric. Do we really think that the majority of those worshippers were pious and/or devout? I think that would be naive.

Some Scots who enjoyed Sundays but who would never regard themselves as hard-line Sabbatarians might say we have almost lost what was a quiet day, a chance to reflect on the week just gone and the business of the week ahead, an opportunity to think of others for once before ourselves. There is a grain of truth in that.

Fundamentalists would pray really hard then argue that the steady move away from Sunday observance is a sure sign of a society plunging into terminal decline – like the Roman Empire, we are on a slippery slope. We may indeed be on that slope – the cause of devout Sabbatarianism is already lost forever.

Most people today would say that Sunday is at last a day of genuine recreation in Scotland. For centuries in other countries on holy days the crowds turned out in public places for fun. In Scotland I suspect most people couldn't wait to get back to work on Monday to escape the mind-numbing drabness that the Sabbath became.

Faith Sangster
Author of *Reclaiming Sunday*, The Retreat, Upperknockity, Buchan, Aberdeenshire

Perhaps, even at the beginning of the twentieth century, James Cameron Lees had the rights of it in his little ditty on churchgoing:

> Some goes to church just for a walk,
> Some goes there to laugh and talk;
> Some go there the time to spend,
> Some go there to meet a friend;
> Some go there for speculation,
> Some go there for observation;
> Some go there to doze and nod,
> It's few goes there to worship God . . .

The world has changed and I for one believe that the freeing of Sunday from the Sabbatarian straightjacket is a massive step forward. People will come to God through the supermarket checkout, at the counter of the public bar, in the passenger lounge on the Harris ferry and on the football terracing. And it is our experience that once they are free to make what they can of the day they will then look to have half an hour of peace and quiet in their nearest church. Mark my words.

Willie Smith
Leader, The New Church of Mammon, Garscube Road, Glasgow (most credit cards taken)

I suspect that Pastor Willie Smith knows perfectly well, as the man who introduced pinball machines in the vestry, that people will no longer come to church unless there is an incentive. The introduction of neon church signs, post-sermon bingo, big screens for the Sky TV Sunday matches has unsurprisingly brought people back into the church, but so much has been lost in trying to be trendy. As for the 'habit' of churchgoing – was there so much wrong with a bit of discipline in our lives, a brief opportunity to consider quietly how fortunate we are and to think of others for just a wee while?

The Rev. Murdo Pine
The Church of Spiritual Rest (Enduring),
Paradise Row, Wishaw

Index